Nordic Walking

Outdoor Adventures

Malin Svensson
Nordic Walking USA

HUMAN KINETICS

Library of Congress Cataloging-in-Publication Data

Svensson, Malin, 1961-
Nordic walking / Malin Svensson.
p. cm. -- (Outdoor adventures)
Includes bibliographical references.
ISBN-13: 978-0-7360-7739-2 (soft cover)
ISBN-10: 0-7360-7739-1 (soft cover)
1. Fitness walking. I. Title.
GV502.S94 2009
613.7'176--dc22

ISBN-10: 0-7360-7739-1 (print)   ISBN-10: 0-7360-8760-5 (Adobe PDF)
ISBN-13: 978-0-7360-7739-2 (print)   ISBN-13: 978-0-7360-8760-5 (Adobe PDF)

Copyright © 2009 by Human Kinetics, Inc.

The Web addresses cited in this text were current as of December 17, 2008, unless otherwise noted.

Acquisitions Editor: Gayle Kassing, PhD; **Developmental Editor:** Melissa Feld; **Assistant Editor:** Rachel Brito; **Copyeditor:** Jan Feeney; **Proofreader:** Jim Burns; **Permissions Manager:** Martha Gullo; **Graphic Designer:** Nancy Rasmus; **Graphic Artist:** Dawn Sills; **Cover Designer:** Keith Blomberg; **Photographer (cover):** Neil Bernstein; **Photographer (interior):** Neil Bernstein, unless otherwise noted. See photo credits on page 197. **Photo Asset Manager:** Laura Fitch; **Visual Production Assistant:** Joyce Brumfield; **Photo Production Manager:** Jason Allen; **Art Manager:** Kelly Hendren; **Associate Art Manager:** Alan L. Wilborn; **Illustrator:** Tim Shedelbower (map on page 73); **Printer:** United Graphics

Printed in the United States of America   10 9 8 7 6 5 4 3 2 1

Human Kinetics
Web site: www.HumanKinetics.com

United States: Human Kinetics
P.O. Box 5076
Champaign, IL 61825-5076
800-747-4457
e-mail: humank@hkusa.com

Canada: Human Kinetics
475 Devonshire Road Unit 100
Windsor, ON N8Y 2L5
800-465-7301 (in Canada only)
e-mail: info@hkcanada.com

Europe: Human Kinetics
107 Bradford Road
Stanningley
Leeds LS28 6AT, United Kingdom
+44 (0) 113 255 5665
e-mail: hk@hkeurope.com

Australia: Human Kinetics
57A Price Avenue
Lower Mitcham, South Australia 5062
08 8372 0999
e-mail: info@hkaustralia.com

New Zealand: Human Kinetics
Division of Sports Distributors NZ Ltd.
P.O. Box 300 226 Albany
North Shore City
Auckland
0064 9 448 1207
e-mail: info@humankinetics.co.nz

This book is dedicated to three wise Nordic ancestors: my grandmother, Farmor Lowa, who, regardless of the weather, walked every day to our house for afternoon coffee; my father, Benkt-Ingvar Svensson, who would be very proud to know I promote our Swedish heritage in America as a way of contributing to a more physically active continent; and my mother, Lena W.-Svensson, who continues to be my role model by continuing to bike, walk, swim, and lift weights in her 80s!

Contents in Brief

Contents

Preface

In this book you will find a well-kept secret from Sweden, Finland, Norway, Denmark, and Iceland: Nordic walking—that is, walking with poles. By simply adding poles and a certain technique to your walking routine, you gain benefits beyond your dreams. You also burn more calories—up to 46 percent! And even though the body is working harder, it does not feel like more of an effort. You also get a full-body workout. Nordic walking is an endurance sport that offers an upper-body strength workout as well. To top it off, it's a low-impact exercise. Nordic walking is derived from cross-country skiing, which is the most beneficial endurance sport in the world. But to Nordic walk, you don't need the snow or the skis to achieve similar benefits. Today the technique has been modified as an enhancement of natural walking and a way to avoid injuries. So anyone can Nordic walk:

- People with balance problems (elderly, rehabilitation patients, those with multiple sclerosis)
- People who need to take weight off the joints (obese people, rehabilitation patients, pregnant women, those with ankle, knee, and hip problems)
- People who find regular walking too easy (fitness enthusiasts)
- Families searching for an activity that each member can participate in
- People who want to find a fun and healthy way to get fit and to stay in shape
- People who want to vary their training for a walking event
- People who want a high-intensity exercise, like running, but with low impact
- Athletes seeking variation in off-season training

This book teaches all you need to know to learn basic Nordic walking and build on the technique to intensify the workouts. You will understand the versatility of this sport because of one little thing: the asphalt paw. It is like a shoe that covers the spike tip at the end of the pole. By keeping the paw on or removing it, you can vary your options in Nordic walking routes and terrain: sidewalks in the city, city parks, beaches, trails in the mountains or deserts, and snow and ice in the winter. You can basically start Nordic walking right outside your door. Imagine no more driving to exercise!

This book reveals the Nordic walking secret and all its benefits to anyone who can walk. Today's society offers increased conveniences to the point where we don't have to leave the house to make a living. So we need an exercise option that is easy and efficient for maintaining health. Nordic walking serves as a very productive and efficient exercise. Sitting indoors takes away the great pleasure of being outdoors. Nordic walking takes you outdoors and close to nature where you can rejuvenate.

This book is divided into two parts. Part I prepares you for Nordic walking. Part II teaches you the techniques and skills so you can use the poles correctly and reap all the benefits. Chapter 1 is an introduction to Nordic walking, its history, and its benefits. Chapter 2 takes you through some fitness exercises and other suggestions for staying fit and focused on Nordic walking year-round. As with any sport, you need specific equipment; chapter 3 covers everything you need to know. When you're ready to Nordic walk, it's always good to get ideas about where you can go, which is covered in chapter 4. You might think that a trail in the mountains is your only option. But after you read the specific suggestions, you'll think about several places in and around your own community as well as around the world that are ideal for Nordic walking. You might even plan a Nordic walking vacation. Chapter 5 covers safety, whether you're walking in the city or in the mountains.

Part II covers Nordic walking techniques and workouts. Chapter 6 starts with the basics so you can get outdoors as soon as possible to try those new poles. To get more benefits from the sport, you can train as you would for any endurance sport. The workout structure is described in chapter 7. After a few weeks, you may want to learn more about how you can intensify the workouts, and the suggestions in chapter 8 will take you to another level—urban Nordic walking—even though you are still Nordic walking within the city limits. Chapter 9 takes the workout to yet another level by adding pole techniques for Nordic trail walking. Maybe it will require some more time, but it will be worth it. Being outdoors close to nature for a couple of hours will recharge your batteries and get you ready for another productive work week.

Three levels of Nordic walking are discussed in this book. Chapter 6 discusses the basic technique, which is considered level 1. Chapter 8 takes you to level 2, urban Nordic walking. Chapter 9 describes level 3, Nordic trail walking. Each level advances the workout. Remember, though, that you can do any level in any environment. For the purposes of this book, the levels have been placed in different environments to show you how you can vary your workout.

In each chapter, you will find safety, consumer, technique, and Nordic walker tips. And after reading a chapter, test your knowledge by answering the questions in the Success Checks at the end of the book. In the appendixes, you will find resources on equipment and anything that relates to Nordic walking.

Writing this book and developing it with the team at Human Kinetics have been wonderful experiences. I hope that you will have an enriched experience walking the Nordic way. Remember to bring some friends along—it makes the journey so much more fun!

Acknowledgments

Making this book happen was a team effort, and I want to thank the following people:

Todd Raymond Smith for all the love and support and for always believing in me. Pål Svensson (my brother in Sweden) and Henrik Boström (my brother-in-law in Finland) for convincing me to bring Nordic walking to America in December 2001.

Gayle Kassing at Human Kinetics for asking me to write this book and for always being there to answer questions and to guide me. Melissa Feld at Human Kinetics for making the editing (and photo) process smooth and enjoyable. The rest of the wonderful and talented Human Kinetics team: Jason Allen, Neil Bernstein, Keith Blomberg, Rachel Brito, Joyce Brumfield, Jan Feeney, Rebecca Fink, Laura Fitch, Lisa Floyd, Martha Gullo, Kelly Hendren, Alexis Koontz, John Laskowski, Jennifer Mulcahey, Nancy Rasmus, Tim Shedlebower, Dawn Sills, Katie Walden, and Al Wilborn.

All the contributing authors of chapter 4: Gary Johnson of the United States; Paula Artley, Alastair Campbell, Suzanne Campbell, and Marilyn Inch of Canada; June Stevenson of New Zealand; and Naohiro Takahashi of Japan.

Todd Raymond Smith for making the photo shoot possible and professional. Lovisa Larsson (my niece from Sweden) for all her love, help, and patience. Shannon Collins at Peak Performance for the use of the beautiful studio. Neil Bernstein for taking great photos and for being so patient. All the enduring and talented models: Nina Hauser, Tara Lynn Thompson, Jack Thompson, Trey Murphy, Mikel-Claire Penick, Anthony Alba, Diane Bishop, Ken Bishop, Anne Yaple, Trinie Valdez, and Suzanne Bogert. And my loyal and loving friends and "family": Neil, Lisa, Alexander, and Mikaela Wessel.

All the manufacturers that sponsored the photo shoot by providing us with the best Nordic walking poles, shoes, clothes, and accessories: Exel, Exerstrider, Foot Solutions, Gabel, Leki, Swix, Western Pole Company, Fitlee, Polar, Asics, Chung Shi, Lowa, Reebok, Saucony, and Springboost. Triscka Mallia for calling everyone and making sure we had the whole Nordic walking community represented.

Simone Schmidt for consulting and legal guidance. Dani Kiwi Meier for the professional input and advice. Mark Fenton for the inspirational work in promoting walking-friendly communities. Marcy Schwam for believing so passionately in Nordic walking. Karen Asp for spreading the word about Nordic walking via the media.

Preparing for a Nordic Walking Adventure

CHAPTER 1

Introduction to Nordic Walking

All glory comes
from daring
to begin.

Eugene F. Ware

What is your first thought when you see somebody walking with poles? The best comment I ever got was "Are you training for the Olympics?" Actually, yes, when I was 19 years old, but now many years later I'm just enjoying a low-impact form of exercise that gets my heart rate up as high as running would. Walking with one pole has been practiced for probably thousands of years. Unless there is snow, you probably relate to walking with two poles as trekking or hiking in the mountain trails. But using two poles in the streets of Los Angeles, Chicago, or New York? What's wrong with that picture? There is no snow or mountains as far as the eye can see. And they left their skis at home! Why are these people walking with poles in Central Park? Believe me; nothing is wrong with this picture. These people are just applying a *new* pole technique while walking, which is called Nordic walking. When walking without poles, you burn around 300 calories an hour. Nordic walking can increase that close to 50 percent—that is, 450 calories per hour. Maybe those pole people aren't that crazy after all. If you tried it, you would feel the effect right away—the muscles in your upper body are working and getting stronger in each step. It feels so good, like the whole body is working. You are not dreaming—Nordic walking is a full-body workout.

Anything that is new is received with mixed reactions. Some want to try it right away. Others may be more skeptical and wait until others have tried it. If you are the hesitant one, you actually may already have gotten a taste of Nordic walking either by using the elliptical trainer at the gym or by using trekking poles in the mountains. Even though they are all similar in nature (using upper and lower body simultaneously), you will learn why Nordic walking is advantageous. If you need even more proof that Nordic walking works, keep reading about the adventure that 8 million people worldwide enjoy as well as the amazing benefits you will gain. Most of these benefits are supported by studies from renowned research institutes and some by testimonials and experiences from Nordic walkers of various ages and fitness levels.

The usefulness of Nordic walking is infinite because of the removable asphalt paw at the bottom of the pole. Although this asphalt paw is only a small part of the pole, it plays a huge role in the versatility of Nordic walking. Wear it whenever you Nordic walk on hard surfaces like asphalt and cement. Take it off when you're on soft or semi-soft surfaces like sand, grass, or dirt. In the winter, take it off to get a better grip on icy parts. Thus, Nordic walking is a versatile activity not only in regard to *who* can perform it, but also to *where* it can be done. Throughout the book, you will see photos of Nordic walking

CONSUMER TIP

Equip yourself with a pair of poles that have removable asphalt paws and include a pair of snow baskets, and you are ready for any adventure anywhere in any season.

adventures in various locations during various seasons. The ideas are endless; tap into your creativity and find your own favorite Nordic adventure.

What Do the Poles Do?

If you still don't understand why people use poles while walking, do the following simple test. You need only a chair, a table, and two arms. Sit down on a chair by a table and place your left hand (in a fist) on the table (see figure 1.1). Place your right hand (flat) on your abdomen. Press the left fist down into the table and release. Repeat this action of press and release. What happens in the abdomen as you do this action? Yes, it activates. Move the right hand around to the chest, back, and back of the arms. The same thing happens with those muscles. This is why you use poles in Nordic walking: to engage the muscles in the upper body.

Figure 1.1   Nordic walking poles engage all the upper-body muscles.

TECHNIQUE TIP

Plant and maintain the Nordic walking pole at an angle to propel the body forward. The hand is forward in a handshake position while the end of the pole that touches the ground is behind you. Trekking poles, in contrast, are mainly planted vertically to provide balance and support.

Imagine applying this pressure to the poles as you are walking. As you are using those poles, you realize that your speed has increased and that you are flying past people, even runners. Also, joints that might have hurt before suddenly get a break. The poles take the pressure off those aching joints. It's like walking with four legs. That's how humans started out on this earth—walking on all fours, which is the natural way. Through the process of human evolution, the long spine has caused so many problems. But with those two extra legs—two poles, that is—in the hands, you can now protect your spine from pain. The poles become an extension of the arms, so you can walk with four legs again. You will feel the difference. The second you place the poles on the ground, you improve the posture: You push away from gravity. Better posture resolves many problems: achy neck, shoulders, back, and hips.

Instruction on using the poles is a necessary step in learning Nordic walking. After being strapped into the poles, most people place the poles in front for balance and support; some even point the ends forward like the heel of a foot that is engaged in walking. Using the poles as trekking poles gives you support and balance. But using them as Nordic walking poles engages your upper body in the work. If you have ever tried using an elliptical trainer, you know how it engages the upper body. Although the movement is similar on an elliptical trainer and during Nordic walking, your upper body benefits more from Nordic walking. On an elliptical trainer, the arms are bent the whole time, so you primarily work the muscles crossing the shoulder joint—that is, the chest and the back muscles. But the poles allow you to straighten the elbows behind you, thereby shaping the triceps (backs of your arms).

Another difference is that the settings on an elliptical trainer cannot be changed regardless of whether you are six feet tall or five feet tall. The poles are adjusted according to your height. If you are five feet eight inches tall, you would most likely need a 115 cm tall pole. It can either be a one-length pole that already is 115 cm or it can be an adjustable pole if you would like to vary the height.

History and Recent Growth

Every Nordic person probably has a version or two on how Nordic walking came about. One common story is that in the 1930s, Finnish cross-country skiers tried to come up with a way to stay in shape year-round. The method was to become known as Nordic walking. It was refined in the mid 1990s by Risto Kasurinen and Marko Kantaneva, who worked for Matti Heikkilä at the Finnish Sport Institute (Vierumäki) and by Sirpa Arvonen, who worked for the (Finnish) National Association for Recreational Sports (Suomen Latu). In 1997, Exel Oy, a Finnish sport equipment manufacturer, produced the first Nordic walking poles, and the concept of Nordic walking became a real fitness activity and sport. Just 10 years later, in 2007, approximately 8 million people worldwide were Nordic walking.

Two names come up regarding the start of this fitness movement of walking with poles. One is a gentleman named Tuomo Jantunen, who brought Nordic walking into the spotlight by accident. On the day of a ceremonious cross-country skiing event in Finland from Suomen Latu to Helsinki on January 5, 1988, a sudden rain melted all the snow. Instead of canceling the occasion, all participants walked with only the ski poles—the idea of Tuomo Jantunen, the managing director of Suomen Latu. He made it his mission to continue developing this "ski-walking" idea into a sport to be performed by anyone, not just athletes.

Another legend is a man in the United States named Tom Rutlin. He started the walking-with-poles movement in 1985. Like any other successful fitness movement such as Pilates, Feldenkrais, or Alexander technique, it came about due to a need. The Finnish cross-country skiers needed to stay in shape all

Nordic skiing: the idea behind Nordic walking.

year-round, so they explored training with poles during the dry seasons. Rutlin was a competitive runner and Nordic skier who became injured, but refused to stop training because of the philosophy of the time—no pain, no gain. Out of despair and persistence, he grabbed his ski poles and added them to his painful running routine. For the first time, he felt some relief from the pain. As he tried to coax his wife, Wendy, into using the poles, he agreed to just walk with the poles instead of running. Not only was it more pleasant to be training with his wife, but he also had a mind–body experience that made him realize the potential of this simple discovery. He felt more benefits from walking with the poles than from running. Out of necessity, Rutlin developed walking with poles (Exerstriding) into a fitness exercise in the United States.

In 2000, the International Nordic Walking Association (INWA) was founded in Finland by Exel Oy to provide enthusiasts with proper and safe instruction as they used their Nordic walking products. Today INWA, an independent association, focuses on the development of education, providing the latest research and offering an international network of instructors promoting Nordic walking to improve people's health and quality of life. INWA has member organizations in more than 20 countries. Over the years, several other educational organizations have sprung up as well as variations of Nordic walking techniques: the INWA technique, the Exerstriding technique, the Fittrek technique, and the ALFA technique, to name a few. The average person might not even notice the difference. There are various ways to learn Nordic walking, depending on the instructor. The original breakdown of the INWA technique into 10 steps was created by Malin Svensson (Svensson, 2003). It has been revised over the years by the INWA Educational Committee and like any other sport, the technique and teaching methods continue to be polished and further developed.

Benefits of Nordic Walking

Regardless of the technique or the method you choose to use to learn Nordic walking, most likely you will see similar results. Just like anything else, it becomes a personal choice of what feels good and what is good for your body. If something starts hurting, you might want to have your technique, gait, and pole length analyzed by a health and fitness professional.

Health Benefits

The most important aspect of Nordic walking is that it gives you so many health benefits that you probably have not experienced through any other sport or exercise. Maybe you would receive similar benefits from a combination of various sports, but not from one single sport alone—not even cross-country skiing. There are so many positive results from simply adding two poles to your regular walking routine (see sidebar).

Any aerobic sport or exercise you do on a regular basis will provide benefits, especially if you can maintain a certain intensity and duration. The incredible advantage Nordic walking has over regular walking is that at any age and at

REASONS TO ADD POLES TO YOUR WALKING ROUTINE

- Burns 20 to 46 percent more calories
- Increases aerobic capacity even at a slow speed
- Enhances mood
- Increases upper-body strength
- Increases heart rate by 5 to 30 beats per minute
- Takes pressure off the joints
- Decreases neck and shoulder pain and stiffness
- Increases upper-body mobility
- Increases functional capacity
- Feels like less of an effort even though the body works harder
- Improves balance and stability, making it safer to walk
- Improves gait and coordination
- Improves core stability and posture
- Creates a meditative and calming effect

any fitness level, you can increase those benefits further. This is due to the increased intensity made possible by extra muscle recruitment. The muscles in the arms, chest, back, and abdomen make the poles work and move. The beautiful thing is that you don't feel the body working harder because the effort to walk a certain distance at the same speed with or without the poles feels the same. However, during the Nordic walking, the muscles of the upper body are involved and demand more oxygen. The heart has to pump faster to deliver the oxygen-filled blood, which is the reason for the increased heart rate. During this walk with poles, you are now burning more calories than if you'd left your poles at home. So if regular walking does not give you enough of a workout, grab the poles to get that heart rate up to a high enough intensity to improve your aerobic capacity.

According to a study done at the Cooper Institute in Dallas, Texas, Nordic walking burns about 20 percent more calories than regular walking. Dr. Tim Church, medical laboratory director of the Cooper Institute, noted that participants had as much as a 46 percent increase in oxygen consumption and about the same caloric expenditure. The intensity of poling (the better technique as well as the more advanced technique that was applied to raise the intensity; see chapter 6 for basic technique and chapters 8 and 9 to add intensity to your poling) varied among participants and thus produced varied results. It is obvious that correct Nordic walking technique improves the benefits. If you want to burn more calories, grab the poles and polish the Nordic walking technique. How does that difference translate into weight loss? Say that two identical twins walk together four times a week, but one Nordic walks and the other walks without poles. Without changing their food intake, they decide to compete to see who will be the first one to lose the first pound. It will take the Nordic walker two weeks and the regular walker three weeks.

Since you will feel equally tired from walking with or without poles, it will be hard to believe that your body is working harder while Nordic walking. Yes, you will feel your arm muscles working along with the other muscles you felt working during the test of pushing one fist to the table. So you can believe that your upper body will get stronger from Nordic walking, but how can you believe that you will burn more calories and that your heart rate will increase as much as if you were running? Try a heart rate monitor! Use one that you wear as a belt around the lower part of your chest and that is connected to a watch on your wrist, which gives a reading of your pulse. The heart rate monitor will tell you the truth.

Once, a 30-year-old writer walked up a hill twice, first without the poles and then with the poles. The speed and the distance were the same. The result was such a surprise to him that the headlines in the *Los Angeles Times* the next day read, "Nordic walking keeps the intensity on track." Thanks to the heart rate monitor, he could *see* that Nordic walking increased his pulse 30 beats per minute. Did he feel a difference? Nope. If he hadn't worn the heart rate monitor, would he have believed it? Nope! Using a heart rate monitor, you can both see and believe that Nordic walking works.

Decreased Joint Pain

Many Nordic walking students show up with aches and pains, but leave feeling that they have finally found something that reduces the impact on their ankle, knee, and hip joints. Imagine an exercise that decreases the impact on the joints but increases heart rate, calories burned, strength, and flexibility. If you weigh 200 pounds (about 91 kg), you will be able to distribute your weight among two legs and two poles. That's a load off the joints. Poles help reduce joint load in legs during downhill walking. Some students with joint problems are hesitant to go down a hill. But after applying the correct downhill technique in Nordic walking, for the first time they are able to go down a hill without pain. (You can learn the technique in chapter 6.)

The second you place the poles in your hands and apply some pressure on them, you will feel how your posture automatically improves. You should have a slight forward lean as you walk or Nordic walk, but a lot of people, unfortunately, do this by bending the upper back or waist. That is not a good posture. The leaning needs to happen as one unit—a straight line from the ankles to the head, no bending in between. If you have a strong core, this should not be a problem. When you plant the poles, you push into the ground to move forward; you also create a push away from gravity. The poles will not only remind you of keeping good posture, but they will also make it easier. Good posture requires good core activation. Apply the slight lean forward as one unit, and you will keep that core working.

Other common aches and pains will show up in the neck and shoulder area as the result of inactivity and office work. Studies have shown that Nordic walking two or three times a week for 10 to 12 weeks decreases neck and shoulder pain and increases the flexibility in the upper body. Many people walk without swinging their arms; instead the arms appear to be glued to the body. Some people even have a habit of walking with the hands in their pockets, not allowing any movement of the arms. These people may have some coordination problems in the early stages of learning Nordic walking. Normal arm swinging provides balance as well as a slight rotation in the upper body. Since this is the correct way of walking or Nordic walking—a slight rotation in the trunk—you will feel muscles that were once tight start to loosen up. The rotation allows those muscles to go back and forth. Nordic walking also releases tension in the upper-body muscles when you go from planting the pole (tension) to pushing back on the pole and softening the grip (relaxation). And Nordic walking definitely teaches you coordination. Initially you might feel uncoordinated if you don't have the correct rhythm (arm matching opposite leg). After some practice, you will feel your coordination easily improve. This way of moving is also called cross-lateral movement, and studies have shown that it stimulates brain activity and improves the learning process. Next time you need to learn something, go Nordic walking while you study it.

In every walk with nature one receives far more than he seeks.

John Muir

Meditative Benefits

Nordic walking is also very meditative. Every time you place that pole into the ground, you connect with Mother Earth, especially if you use surfaces like grass, sand, and dirt. It's a grounded feeling. The rhythm that you automatically get into will put you on autopilot and rock you into another world. Many yoga practitioners call it walking yoga. The fact that you can do it outdoors and in beautiful environments gives you a nice break from your daily environment. Nordic walking has a calming effect on the mind.

Improved Walking Habits

Nordic walking is an enhancement of regular walking. Even though you have been walking since you were around a year old, a lot of things have happened since then. Your body is an amazing machine, and whatever you tell it to do, it will adjust. If you sit a lot, the upper front thighs will shorten. The opposing muscles will thus compensate to lengthen and sometimes weaken. If you have weak buttocks muscles (opposite to the front thigh muscles, also known as the hip flexors), you may not have the strength to keep your foot arch up every time you put weight on your leg. Basically every time you take a step, the arches collapse and soon the knee and hip will do the same. Suddenly the way you walk may not only be incorrect, but also painful. Learning Nordic walking will give you a chance to learn how to walk again. Don't ignore the simple instructions in chapter 6; embrace them and after increased awareness you actually may walk without pain.

Some people have health conditions that prevent them from walking well or even walking at all. My first success story was a lady from Kansas whom I met by chance while vacationing. She had multiple sclerosis and struggled with walking with some poles, and my intuition told me to approach her. After some instruction with some other poles, she walked around on flat surfaces as well as up and down a hill as if she had been walking fine her whole life. It was a lifesaving moment for her and an affirmation to me that I was on the right track to helping people.

Increased Functional Capacity

Studies show that Nordic walking improves functional capacity in elderly people. An example of a functional movement is sitting down in a chair and standing up. The poles offer balance and stability because they function as two extra legs while walking. Elderly people will feel safer and probably be more prone to walking around, and thus their whole world will change. It doesn't matter at what age you start exercising; you will see and feel the benefits. When it comes to moving and improving your fitness level, the expression "It's never too late" applies. When you look at people using a cane, there is often a limp involved. It is very pronounced when the person walks because there seems to be an imbalance between the right and the left side. Put two poles in their hands, and the limp will either be reduced or disappear.

Have fun—try Nordic walking.

Best of all, Nordic walking makes it more fun to move and exercise, a finding that is based on studies as well as personal accounts. One of my students said, "I never just walk, because that's boring. But Nordic walking is fun because it gives me something to do." And you know that if something is enjoyable, you will stick with it. This is one of the most important factors in today's sedentary society—to find an exercise that you will do on a regular basis to reap the healthy benefits.

What's more, people really enjoy walking together. With the pervasiveness of e-mail communication, you can easily miss out on simple yet crucial face-to-face social interactions. Take advantage of the social health benefits from exercising: Walk with a buddy or in a group, or participate in a charity walk event. Join a Nordic walking class and cover all areas of health—social, mental, and physical.

Any Age, Any Fitness Level

You might be thinking about how you or a friend can benefit from Nordic walking. People who are pregnant, overweight, have lower-body joint pain, or are recovering from foot, knee, or hip surgery all need to take weight off their joints while walking. This is possible via the poles. And anyone who needs

People at any age and any fitness level will benefit from Nordic walking.

help with balance would benefit from the poles. Think about somebody who is elderly or has a debilitating disease such as multiple sclerosis. Can you think of somebody who has a limp or has trouble walking? That person could walk better with poles.

Usually Nordic walking classes offer various techniques at many levels, so anyone of any age or fitness level can gain positive results. Depending on your goal—rehabilitation, health, weight loss, fitness, or sport performance—you can find a technique and level that work for you. If you don't have any injuries and wish to improve your fitness level, try intermediate or advanced levels. If you're an athlete, you can enhance your performance by using plyometric jumps and bouncing exercises with the poles. You can do these exercises in short intervals, which stress the anaerobic energy system. Nordic walking is a great cross-training tool for athletes during the off-season. Regardless of your fitness level, you always need to start with the basic technique in Nordic walking. Any added intensity is built on a solid foundation. In part II, you will learn how to apply ways of intensifying your Nordic walking workout, urban Nordic walking, and Nordic trail walking.

Many Nordic walking pole companies manufacture poles for kids. There has been debate about the appropriate age for learning Nordic walking. One aspect of child development—coordination—suggests that the age of 10 is a good time to introduce the activity. Keep in mind that everyone matures differently, so that's just a general guideline.

Year-Round Nordic Adventures

Once you have learned the basics in Nordic walking, you may get tempted to try other similar physical activities. If there is snow on the ground, apply the Nordic walking technique, covered in part II, to other Nordic sports or fitness activities, such as Nordic winter walking (Nordic walking on compact snow), Nordic snowshoeing (snowshoeing with poles), or classic-style Nordic fitness skiing (cross-country skiing with wider and shorter skis). If the ground is dry, you can go Nordic hiking (hiking with poles). A similar technique can also be applied to Nordic blading, which is in-line skating with poles.

Like Nordic walking and Nordic hiking, Nordic blading can be practiced during spring, summer, fall, and, if you live in a warmer climate, winter. Cross-country skiing is divided into either classic style (legs and arms move forward and back) or skating style (legs move alternating from side to side while both arms plant the poles at the same time). In skating-style Nordic fitness skiing, you use the same pole technique as in Nordic blading—that is, you plant both poles at the same time. This is yet another alternative for the winter season. Having access to so many choices with a common theme—poles—keeps the training fresh and fun. Another advantage of training using the Nordic sport adventures all year is that you don't have to go through a new learning curve in using the poles, and for half of the activities you can even use the same poles. Nordic walking poles are a low-cost investment in staying fit and enjoying outdoor adventures year-round.

NORDIC SPORT ADVENTURES

Spring, Summer, and Fall

- Nordic walking (with Nordic walking poles)
- Nordic hiking (with Nordic walking poles)
- Nordic blading

Nordic walking.

Nordic hiking.

Nordic blading.

Winter

- Nordic winter walking (with Nordic walking poles)
- Nordic snowshoeing (with Nordic walking poles)
- Classic-style Nordic fitness skiing
- Skating-style Nordic fitness skiing

Nordic winter walking safely over icy patches.

Use the Nordic walking poles in the winter—go Nordic snowshoeing!

Cross-country skiing—classic style.

Cross-country skiing—skating style.

CONSUMER TIP

A great accessory is the snow basket: Attach it to the bottom of the pole and hit the snow. Enjoy Nordic winter walking or Nordic snowshoeing.

Conclusion

Nordic walking is not only something new, fun, and easy to try; it is also an experience that will leave a smile on your face when you experience all the benefits for the body, mind, and soul. What other sport requires less effort but gives you more results? What other sport can you perform anywhere and still get a full-body workout? What other tools like the poles provide such variation? On top of that, the versatility of terrain and surface usage is due to a tiny part of the pole—the removable asphalt paw, which is located at the bottom of the pole.

Be creative and go Nordic walking on any surface (asphalt, grass, sand, dirt, snow, and ice), in various terrains (flat, hills, rugged), and in various environments (desert, mountains, beach, city streets). Be daring and try something new, beneficial, and adventurous!

CHAPTER 2

Adventure Fit for Nordic Walking

> Life is like riding a bicycle. To keep your balance you must keep moving.
>
> *Albert Einstein*

Do you want to stay in shape year-round? Try Nordic walking! It's a full-body workout that can be performed outdoors through all four seasons. All you need to know is the basics of Nordic walking, which most people will pick up quickly without any previous training. However, to take the activity a step further, certain muscles need to be strong. The following exercises will help you get ready for the Nordic walking movement as well as keep your body balanced throughout the year. The training components (flexibility, strength, and endurance) all focus on the motion of Nordic walking. In other words, the exercises are sport specific. Examples of cross-training activities are presented toward the end of this chapter. All the activities in the Nordic sport adventures (Nordic blading, Nordic fitness skiing, cross-country skiing, Nordic snowshoeing, and Nordic winter walking) are discussed along with other common endurance sports. The motivational factor is a given, but maybe another more important reason to do cross-training is to stay injury free.

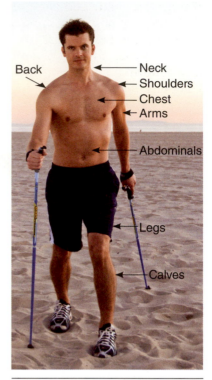

Nordic walking is a full-body workout.

Get a Balanced Body

People tend to train their bodies according to what they need in order to perform a certain sport or activity. The exercises in this chapter stress the various components of fitness (flexibility, strength, and endurance) to support the physical skills needed for Nordic walking. In addition to the specific results from each segment, there are other automatic gains. You can intensify each strengthening exercise to add other benefits, such as balance. Coordination will automatically happen through the Nordic walking technique itself. Though balance may seem like something only an elderly person would need to practice, you would be surprised at how balance training can add challenges to your workout. Any athlete will testify to how important balance training is in strength training. As a child, you don't think about it. If you've had the privilege of challenging your body through speed, agility, flexibility, strength, endurance, coordination, and balance activities on a playground, you have built a sturdy foundation for life.

Chapter 6 presents pointers on walking correctly to build a better understanding of a basic walking technique. If you have access to a health and fitness professional (such as a physical therapist) who can analyze your gait, that person's observations can be easily incorporated into your strength and flexibility training program. You most likely have muscle imbalances, and if those are addressed early on, you can avoid injuries. Walking and sitting-and-standing motions (squats) are basic movements and wonderful tools for detecting compensations.

Place a chair in front of a mirror and check your form. See if you can detect any abnormal movement (deviations) when you sit or stand up. A common compensation is collapsing in your knees when you sit down. This can be a sign of weak buttocks muscles. In your strength training program, you would focus on exercises that strengthen the buttocks muscles.

SAFETY TIP
Good Form

Whether you are sitting, standing, or moving, it is important that you maintain good posture. When you start loading your body with weight, this becomes even more imperative. Keep these three basic instructions in mind for all training components:

1. Keep the abdominal muscles lightly pulled in.
2. Keep the shoulders gently back and down.
3. Keep the body even and aligned.

Good form while moving the body.

Common deviations such as (a) knees caving in, (b) leaning forward too much, and (c) hiked shoulders.

Flexibility for Nordic Walking

When you think of flexibility, you might think about having tight muscles, especially the hamstrings. As a result, you get into a position that is uncomfortable, so you don't stay there more than 10 seconds, and those hamstrings get all the attention because you can feel how tight they are. Stop! This is not a good approach. No wonder people regard flexibility as something painful and unnecessary.

If you knew why flexibility is a key ingredient in physical fitness, you would change your mind. The easiest way to describe flexibility is to say that you are able to bend without breaking anything. According to NASM (National Academy of Sports Medicine), flexibility is the normal extensibility of all soft tissues that allows the full range of motion of a joint (see figure 2.1). Soft tissue is muscles, tendons, and ligaments. They are all directly or indirectly connected to joints or bones. A joint is a junction of bones where movement occurs. Take a moment to check some of your joints: Circle the ankle, bend the knee, circle the wrist, and bend the elbow. Ligaments connect bone to bone to provide stability or limit range of motion in the joint. A tendon is the extension of a muscle, and it is the part that attaches to a bone. When the muscle performs (shortens), the bone to which it is connected via a tendon will move. If the muscle is a boat, the tendon is its anchor. Do a biceps curl (see figure 2.2). In other words, move the hand toward the shoulder. You have to bend the elbow to make this possible. The

Figure 2.2 Muscles attach to bones. Muscles move the bones. The biceps (front arm) muscle moves the bones of the forearm.

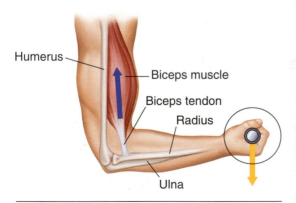

Figure 2.1 The health of the soft tissue—muscles, tendons, and ligaments—determines the health of the joint.

biceps muscle (front of the upper arm) shortens and brings the whole forearm toward you. Remember the anchor—the biceps tendon attaches (anchors) on the bone of the forearm. Your body was made to move; otherwise you would not have joints.

Why Do You Need Flexibility Training?

By now, you probably see how important it is to take joints into account when you think about flexibility. Imagine opening a door. If the hinges have full range, you can open the door fully. If something was wrong with the door, it would affect the hinge and you would not be able to open the door fully. The hinge works as a joint. The door works similar to the muscles, ligaments, and tendons: If they are all normal lengths, the joints would move normally. Different joints require different ranges of motion. Check your knee—bend and extend it. Now, check your wrist, which you can actually circle as well as bend and extend. So muscles around the joint need to be at a perfect length to allow that specific joint to move optimally. There are various degrees of flexibility. You can actually be at equal risk for injuries if your soft tissues are too tight or too loose. Tight muscles will limit the range of motion of a joint and thus they need to be stretched. Imagine having very tight muscles in the front of your thigh (hip flexors). Exaggerate the tightness so much that when you get up from a sitting position, you are able to stand up only halfway. Now imagine walking like that. The body is an adaptable machine, so it will adjust and allow you to walk like that, but at what cost? Soon the back will complain and say, "Hey, stop that position. I was not made to work this way. I will go on strike unless you make a change." What's a solution? Stretch the front muscles (hip flexors) and give the back a break.

Soft tissues can also be too long; that is classified as hyperextension of a joint. Think of rhythmic gymnasts and some extremely flexible ballet dancers. You might say, "Oh, I wish I was as flexible." But think again. Their ligaments are often too stretched, and the joints those ligaments are connected to need stability instead of additional flexibility. Their range of motion is abnormal—too much, in fact. So be cautious when you stretch so you can avoid overstretching.

Stretching to Achieve Flexibility

Stretching is the way to increase or maintain flexibility. There are three ways you can stretch (trigger release, dynamic stretching, and static stretching); each one has a specific purpose.

Trigger Release

If you have a knot on a rope, what happens if you keep pulling the rope? The knot gets tighter. When you apply this analogy to your body, you will soon realize that holding a stretch may not always get the knot in your muscle to release. And you need to release it because it prevents the muscle from working or functioning at 100 percent of its capacity. So if regular stretching won't do the trick, then trigger release might work. This is an optional but recommended type of stretching.

Trigger release can be compared to acupressure: You find specific points on the body that are tight (tense), have a knot, or are sensitive to the touch, and you apply pressure with your fingers, hand, or elbow. Muscle tension is released and blood circulation is increased. Think of the knot as a dead end filled with trash. When you release the knot, the fresh blood will be able to run through and get the trash out. The formerly knotted part of the muscle can now work properly.

Instead of using your hand, you can use a foam roller. You can either put your body weight on it while leaning against a wall (foam roller in between you and the wall), or lie down on the floor with the foam roller under you (the method shown in this book). Sometimes a tennis ball can be used on muscles that can take deeper and more pointed pressure, such as the buttocks. It all depends on your sensitivity. You need to determine whether it works for you. If you feel pain that makes your teeth clench, you are doing yourself a disservice. The muscles will tense instead of giving in. Move around and explore how you can take the weight off the foam roller to diminish the pressure. The discomfort from the pressure should allow you to breathe normally and relax. It should *feel good* when the point of discomfort gives in a little. Keep in mind that there will not be a 100 percent release. Look and feel for only a slight change. Remember to stop doing trigger release if it has the reverse effect—if the pain increases.

As always, ask a physician if trigger release is something you should do. If you have osteoporosis, trigger release with a foam roller is not recommended.

TECHNIQUE TIP
Trigger Release

Purpose: Release tension in the muscles.
Order: Before the dynamic stretching—part of the warm-up.
Instructions:

- Move around slowly on the foam roller until you find a point of some discomfort in the muscle.

- Hold the position until there is a change.

- Move to the next point.

- If no change has occurred within 30 seconds, move on to the next point.

- If the pressure pain increases instead of decreases, move on to another point.

TRIGGER RELEASE ON THE CALVES AND HAMSTRINGS (BACK OF THE LEG)

Place the roller under the ankle. Scoot forward while your calf rolls over the foam roller *(a)*. Move the foam roller gently over the back of the knee and continue rolling the foam roller up the back of your leg until you reach the buttock muscle *(b)*. Explore by turning the foot *in* and then *out* to feel different aspects of the muscles. To apply more pressure, cross the other leg over the working leg. Repeat on the other leg.

TRIGGER RELEASE ON THE BUTTOCKS

Place the foam roller under the buttocks. Bend both knees and keep both feet on the floor. Shift your weight over to the right buttock only. Then cross the right leg over the left leg. Repeat on the left buttock.

TRIGGER RELEASE ON THE BACK

Place the roller crosswise under the midback. Lift the hips up so the back is parallel with the floor. Move in between the rib cage—move the roller from the midback to the shoulders. Don't let the roller go below the rib cage. Keep hands lightly behind the head to support the neck. Explore bringing the elbows together and apart to feel various aspects of the muscles.

TRIGGER RELEASE ON OUTSIDE OF THE LEG

Lie on one side with the foam roller under your upper hip *(a)*. Roll down to just above the knee *(b)*. Explore by turning the hip toward the floor and away from the floor to feel different aspects of the muscles. Repeat on the other leg. If this is your least favorite exercise of them all, you are not alone. However, this is often the area of the body that needs the most work.

TRIGGER RELEASE ON OUTSIDE OF THE LOWER LEG

Lie on one side. Start with the foam roller under the knee *(a)*. Roll down to the ankle *(b)*. Repeat on the other leg.

TRIGGER RELEASE ON THE QUADRICEPS

Lie facedown with the roller placed high beneath the hip. Keep the other leg off the roller and bent to the side in a frog position. Slowly roll down toward the knee. Explore by turning the foot in as you roll back up to the hip. Repeat on the other leg.

Dynamic Stretching

Before you start working out (walking, running, or lifting weights), it is always a good idea to increase your body temperature, get the blood circulating, loosen the muscles, and improve the joint functions to prepare the body for physical activity. If you plan to go for a walking workout, then start with some gentle *dynamic* stretches (see chapter 7) (not to be confused with *static* stretches!). Then continue to walk slowly for 5 to 10 minutes before you increase the walking speed and intensity. If you plan to do a strength workout, the warming up order can change to first getting on the elliptical trainer or a treadmill for an easy 5-10 minute warm-up. Then continue warming up with some dynamic stretches that target the movement and muscles you are about to use during the strength training exercises. Studies indicate that strength decreases right after static stretching, so make sure you follow the instructions on performing the dynamic movements.

Dynamic stretching involves body movements that take the joints through the full range of motion. An example is a supine ball stretch, (see Bend–Extend on the Ball photo, page 29) in which you lie faceup on a stability ball and move from a bent position to one in which your body extends fully, which works the muscles from the ankles to the shoulders. This pattern is repeated about 10 to 20 times; the whole time the joints are slightly challenged into an increasing but still comfortable range of motion. Move as deep as the muscles around the joint allow because of their length; otherwise the dynamic stretching exercise will hurt you more than help you.

Dynamic stretching will not increase the length in the muscle. To lengthen muscles, you need to do static stretching. Dynamic stretching can also be compared to functional movements that you want to ensure you can maintain throughout your adult life. For example, sitting down and getting up (squatting) is something you want to be able to do without support or compensation. If your calf muscles are too tight as you sit down, your feet most likely will respond by rotating out. In other words, the ankle joint does not allow the full movement of sitting down without having to compensate. This is called muscular imbalance. Trigger release and static stretching on the calf muscles will release and lengthen the muscles.

It is very common for athletes to use dynamic stretching as part of their warm-up before an event. Most likely those movements will look more exaggerated (yet controlled) than the ones shown in the photos. The dynamic movements used here are quite gentle in nature, like a nice awakening of the body. You can make each movement easier or harder according to your capabilities, limitations, and flexibility. The idea is to start with a range of motion that feels comfortable and then increase it if your body approves. Listen to your body! Stop if you feel pain.

TECHNIQUE TIP
Dynamic Stretching

Purpose: Warm up the muscles and joints to prepare the body for the activity to be performed.

Order: Before the workout—part of the warm-up *(Optional: Before a strength training workout, add an easy 5 to 10 minutes on an elliptical trainer or treadmill prior to the dynamic stretching).*

Instructions:

- Practice good form (review the three reminders in the safety tip at the beginning of this chapter).
- Gently move the joint in a comfortable range of motion.
- Increase the range of motion if the body allows.
- Move in a controlled manner.
- Repeat each movement 10 times on each joint.

OPPOSITE ARM AND LEG LIFT

Get into an all-fours position on a soft mat *(a)*. (You should look like a table.) The back is straight and the head is lined up with the spine. The shoulder joints are in line with the wrists. The hip joints are lined up with the knee joints. Keep the abdomen slightly pulled in the whole time as you exhale and lift the right arm and the left leg simultaneously. Extend the right arm forward and the left leg back *(b)*. Pause at the top for three counts. Inhale and slowly lower the limbs. Repeat the movement using alternate arm and leg. Keep the height of the lift in line with the back.

BEND–EXTEND ON THE BALL

Sit on a stability ball. Walk the feet out in front of you as you sink down with the buttocks toward the floor *(a)*. The back and head are supported by the ball. Feet are on the floor and knees are bent. Exhale and roll back on the ball by straightening the legs until you are balancing on the heels. Reach back with the arms *(b)*. Hold for three counts and then slowly return to the bending position. Repeat the movement.

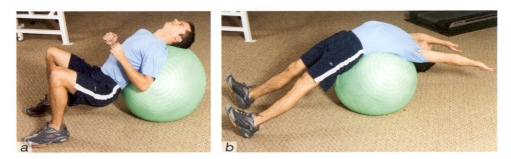

CLOCK LUNGE

Stand in an open space, which allows you to lunge out in every direction. Pretend you are standing in the middle of a clock. Step forward with one foot (plant the heel firmly) to 12 o'clock and lunge as far as it feels comfortable *(a)*. Return. Step sideways to 3 o'clock and lunge as far as it feels comfortable *(b)*. Return. Step backward to 6 o'clock, keeping the heel off the floor *(c)*. Lunge and return. Repeat the same thing with alternate leg (12, 3, and 6 o'clock). Repeat the whole routine three times.

ANKLE CIRCLES AND OVERHEAD

Stand on one leg. Opposite foot is slightly off the floor. Circle the ankle in both directions *(a)* as the arms straighten as they rise toward the ceiling *(b)*, and bend as they come toward the floor. Change legs and repeat.

Static Stretching

This last type of stretching is also performed last—at the end of the workout. Although it is the most well-known type of stretching, it is unfortunately often misplaced as part of the warm-up instead of as part of the cool-down. As mentioned previously, studies indicate that static stretching before a workout will decrease the strength in the muscles. As you can imagine, this is not a good starting place if you lift weights. Unless static stretching is prescribed by a health professional

TECHNIQUE TIP

Static Stretching

Purpose: Stretch the muscles to their original length or farther if needed.
Order: After the workout—part of the cool-down.
Instructions:

- Practice good form (review the three reminders at the beginning of this chapter).
- Get into a correct position (check the photos).
- Stretch the muscle until you feel a mild discomfort (tension).
- On every exhalation, feel tension decrease in the muscle.
- Hold the position for 30 seconds.
- Gently ease out of the stretch.

for the beginning of a workout, make sure you use these static stretches *after* the workout.

Inside the muscles and tendons are receptors that report changes in muscles' length and tension. When you first get into a stretch position, some receptors send a message to the brain that the muscle is being stretched. The brain responds by sending a message to the muscle to stop this stretch by contracting. When a muscle contracts, it means that it actually shortens. That is not the effect you are looking for; your goal is to lengthen the muscle. But there is a way to trick the brain. If you maintain the position long enough, other receptors (the ones that respond to tension) send a message for help to the brain that there is too much tension in the muscle. Now the brain has to send an *opposite* message to the muscle—to relax! It's important to hold each static stretch for 30 seconds to lengthen the muscle.

TENT STRETCH

This stretch is a well-known yoga pose called downward-facing dog. It works so many parts of the body and is thus a very productive stretch. Start on the floor on all fours *(a)*. Spread the fingers. Activate the core, exhale, and raise the hips straight up as high as possible by lifting the knees off the floor *(b)*. Get up on your toes to push the hips up higher. You can keep the knees bent. Push through the hands into the floor and try to move the chest closer to the thighs. Don't change positions of the hands or feet. Keep the head in between the arms. The ears should be in line with the arms. Without sacrificing the height of the hips, gently attempt to straighten the legs by activating the front thighs (quads) *(c)*. Now gently let the heels drop toward the floor. If the heels can touch the floor, push the heels down into the floor. Stay in this position for 30 seconds and feel the stretch in the shoulders, back, hamstrings, and calves. Breathe!

CHEST AND ARM STRETCH ON BALL

Sit on a stability ball. Walk the feet out in front of you until you are lying on the ball. The upper back and head are supported by the ball. Feet are on the floor and knees are bent. Ankle joints and knee joints are lined up. Tighten the buttocks and make sure the hips are level with the knees. There should be a straight line from the head to the knees—like a table-top. Open up the chest and bring the arms out to the side. It should look like a T from above. Gently push the shoulder blades into the ball. Open up the hands. Hold for 30 seconds and feel the stretch in the chest and arms.

CHEST, SHOULDER, AND BACK STRETCH ON THE BALL

Stay in the same position as in the previous stretch, but move the arms: Bring them together until they are shoulder-width apart. From there, lower them slowly behind you. It's easy to arch the lower back, but make sure the core stays engaged. Also keep the arms straight (no bending in the elbows) to get a beneficial stretch for the shoulder joints. Hold for 30 seconds and feel the stretch in the chest, shoulders, and sides of the back.

HIP FLEXOR STRETCH

Take a long step forward. Both feet are straight and pointing forward. The back should be straight—no lean-ing forward or backward. Feel a slight pull at the top of the front thigh. To increase the stretch, tuck the pelvis under and tighten the buttocks of the leg that is being stretched. Now slowly raise the arms up, keeping the core activated. Palms are facing each other. Hold for 30 seconds and feel the stretch in the upper front thigh. Change legs.

QUADRICEPS STRETCH

Stand in a solid position with feet parallel and slightly apart. Keeping the knees aligned, lift one foot up in back and grab it in back. Gently bring the foot toward the buttocks. Feel the mild discomfort in the quadriceps muscle (front of the thigh). If you have good balance, gently raise the other hand straight up. Hold for 30 seconds and feel the stretch in the quad. Change legs.

Here are some common mistakes in this stretch: The knee points outward (correct form is to point the knee downward), the lower back arches too much (correct form is to tilt the pelvis slightly under to a neutral position and pull the abdomen in slightly to lock the pelvic position), and the whole body tilts (correct form is a tall posture). If you struggle with this stretch, you have other options: Do another quad stretch or hold on to something sturdier.

TRICEPS AND SHOULDER STRETCH

Stand with feet parallel and hip-width apart. Raise one arm straight up and bend the elbow so the hand points down toward the shoulder blades. Put the opposite hand behind your back and bend that arm so that the hand points up toward the shoulder blades. The goal is to have the two hands meet. Hold for 30 seconds and feel the stretch in the back of the arm that is pointing down. Change arms.

Strength Training for Nordic Walking

One of the best benefits of Nordic walking is an increase in upper-body strength. After your first Nordic walking session, you will feel those triceps muscles. As mentioned earlier, many people have weak and unbalanced muscles. You will definitely get stronger by doing Nordic walking, but you can also speed up the process by doing some additional strengthening exercises.

Why Do You Need Strength Training?

You most likely already do some type of aerobic exercise (walking, running, biking, or swimming), but most people aren't as likely to integrate strength training into workout routines. Even more people skip the warm-up or cool-down stretches. Hopefully that will change.

• **Improve bone mass.** Between the ages of 20 and 30, most people have the maximal amount of bone mass they will ever have—that is, at this stage of life, the skeleton is at its strongest. After that it will decline. Strength training and weight-bearing exercises such as walking can delay the loss of bone mass because when you challenge a muscle, it will stimulate the bone to which it attaches. The challenge will differ because of age and fitness level. For children and adolescents, walking may not provide enough stimuli, but running and jumping will do the trick. For fit people, the strength training program has to be more challenging than for novices or deconditioned people. It is important to build and maintain strong bone mass at any age, but especially as you enter midlife, so that you can prevent osteoporosis (severe bone loss), which makes the bones more susceptible to fractures. The skeleton is your frame, so build a sturdy one.

• **Improve muscle mass and appearance**. Think of your body weight as divided into fat mass and fat-free mass. Any body tissue not containing fat is fat free, such as muscle, bone, and water. A certain amount of fat is essential in order for the body to function properly. Other than that, the goal is to increase the fat-free (muscle) mass and thus decrease the fat. Just like bone mass, muscle mass declines around age 30—mainly as a result of decreased physical activity. The result—an increase in body fat—is not desirable for your health. That is why it is crucial to stick to an adequately intense strength training program. Strong and lean muscles will not only look good but will also help your body function better and thus enable you to maintain your functional independence.

• **Improve functional abilities.** Whether you pick up your kids or carry groceries up the stairs, these activities will get easier if you do resistance training two or three times a week. Kids and young adults who build a strong foundation of fitness will benefit in their later years. Today's generation of kids and young adults will most likely have aches and pains as adults unless they are encouraged to strengthen their young bodies.

Designing the Workout

Different types of strength training yield different results: A bodybuilder must work out differently than a marathon runner would. A competitive bodybuilder is judged by the mass, definition, and the balance of the muscles. Extremely heavy weightlifting for a small number of repetitions, sometimes only one to three, can be the training scheme for the desired results. On the opposite end of the spectrum is the marathon runner, who cannot have too much muscle mass. It would be inefficient to carry a heavy and muscular body for 26 miles. A marathon runner's strength program would involve weights that are heavy enough to fatigue the muscle after 10 to 15 repetitions. So the difference lies in the amount of load, repetitions, and sets you perform. Nordic walking is an endurance sport, so it focuses on strengthening the muscles used in the sport as well as training the types of movements used in the sport.

To get the desired results from strength training, you need to load the muscles enough so that they become fatigued after a certain number of repetitions. As you get stronger, you need to adjust the weight and number of repetitions. Strength training can involve using your own body weight, free weights, resistance bands, or machines at the gym. If you don't have the equipment shown in the photos, apply the alternative suggestions. It is important to use proper form to avoid injuries. If you are a novice, you may want to hire a trainer for a session. You can show the trainer the photos of the exercises you want to perform.

The goal is to perform 15 repetitions in each exercise. If you can perform more, increase the weight. If you can't do 15, decrease the weight. If you do the same exercise more than once, then rest a minute or less in between the sets. Correct breathing will make the exercise easier because of the rhythm you create. With proper core activation (pelvis locked in neutral position by gently pulling in the abdominal muscles), the exhalation phase will give you extra strength to lift the weight. Practice the following breathing rhythm: Exhale during the heavy phase—usually away from gravity. Inhale during the easier phase—usually when you return the weight to the starting position. How fast or slow you lift the weight makes a difference. Start with an even speed (two or three seconds) up and down. When you feel comfortable with the proper form, use more speed in the heavy phase, pause at the top, and control the weight as you return to the start position. You basically divide the exercise into three phases: fast (power), stop (pause), slow (control). Plan to do the exercises two or three times a week with at least one day of recovery in between each session.

Progression and Variation

To avoid boredom and plateaus, vary the training as well as the exercises. Start by doing one set twice a week; if you can keep the schedule, increase to two sets in your third week. If your body agrees, increase to three sets in your sixth week. After the second week, you're probably stronger and can increase the

INSTRUCTIONS FOR STRENGTH TRAINING

- Train 2 or 3 times a week.
- At least 1 day recovery.
- Do 10 to 15 repetitions.
- Do 1 to 3 sets.
- Rest 1 minute or less.
- Use an even speed (2 or 3 seconds) up and down.
- Exhale away from gravity; inhale toward gravity.
- Use proper form to avoid injuries.

weight. Remember, if you can perform more than 15 repetitions, increase the weight; if you can't do 15 repetitions, decrease the weight.

Start with an exercise that is simple to perform. When you feel comfortable with your form and ability, make it more difficult by adding something unstable to stand on. Then change your position to staggered (one foot in front of the other with feet still hip-width apart), followed by standing on one leg. As you increase the difficulty of the leg position, make sure the ankle stays strong to benefit from the progression. If the ankle keeps caving in (pronation), go back to the previous stance. A more complex exercise is more difficult, but you have to be honest with yourself and judge it objectively. If you are all over the place, you need to take it down a level. Challenge yourself *only* if you are able to maintain proper form throughout all repetitions; otherwise you will injure yourself.

Another way to vary your workouts is circuit training. This works best after you have familiarized yourself with the exercises, probably after four to six sessions or two to three weeks. After you have performed one exercise for 10 to 15 repetitions, you move directly to another exercise and so on until you have finished all exercises. That is one set. Take a break and have some water. If you have progressed to two sets, do another one in the same fashion.

Athletes follow programs that are sometimes planned years in advance. Each program is broken down to a year, months, and weeks. Every two- to four-week period has a specific purpose and thus the training shifts greatly in order to avoid training plateaus. In a similar way, you can create a variation not only between workouts, but also between weeks. The first week can be the easy one with weight heavy enough so you can do 15 repetitions. The second week can be circuit training and a weight load that is heavy enough for you to perform 12 repetitions. In the third week, you can do all three sets back to back with no more than one minute of rest between each set (same exercise three times). Try a weight that makes you fatigued after 10 repetitions. Here

PROGRESSION FOR STRENGTH TRAINING

- Vary speed: power, pause, control.
- Get less rest in between each set or each exercise.
- Increase weight.
- Increase repetitions (maximum 15).
- Increase sets (maximum 3).
- Stand on an unstable surface.
- Stand in a staggered position.
- Stand on one leg.
- Do circuit training.
- Vary workouts and intensity from week to week.

is another structure for this last workout: First set is 15 repetitions, second set 12, and third 10. Adjust the weight accordingly for each set.

Everything depends on how your body is adapting. When you have consistency, no pain, and no injuries, you can experiment more when you have built your base. If, on the other hand, you have the opposite (inconsistency, pain, and injuries), then rest and resume slowly when you have fully recovered. Consider hiring a certified personal trainer who can design a program using the suggested exercises as well as checking your form to avoid injuries. If your budget is limited, you can hire a trainer for a few sessions to design a customized program and to check your form so it becomes automatic when you work on your own. Set up follow-up sessions with the trainer so that he or she can check in every two weeks or every month to make sure you stay on track.

Remember the three elements of good form from page 21:

1. Keep the abdominal muscles lightly pulled in.
2. Keep the shoulders gently back and down.
3. Keep the body even and aligned.

Equipment for the Eight Exercises

- ☐ Stability ball
- ☐ Free weights
- ☐ Resistance band or sport cord (alternative for the gym: cable machine)

INCLINE PUSH-UP (CHEST AND CORE MUSCLES)

With good form, place both hands shoulder-width apart on a sturdy machine or bench. Walk the feet out until you are in a straight-line leaning position *(a)*. Keep feet hip-width apart. Inhale and slowly lean forward as one unit *(b)*; exhale and push back only halfway. Repeat 10 to 15 times.

Easy: Use a higher bench and place feet closer to the higher bench or machine.

Moderate: Walk the feet out farther from the bench (heels will come up as you lean forward) or lower the bench.

Hard: As you lean forward, lift one leg slightly back, leading with the buttock (hip extension). There should be absolutely no pain in the lower back. To make it harder, use a stability ball.

LUNGE (LEG MUSCLES)

Stand with feet hip-width apart. Get into the starting position by taking a step back with the right leg, but balance only on the ball of the right foot *(a)*. Inhale and activate the right buttock and push off into a lunge (land with heel first) *(b)*. This is the end position. Exhale and return to starting position. Repeat 10 to 15 times.

Go down only as far down as the knee and feet allow. Keep good alignment. If it's hard to maintain alignment, don't go as deep on the lunge.

Easy: Lunge down only halfway. Use same leg.

Moderate: Alternate legs. Lunge down so the back knee almost touches the floor. Add the arms to the movement: Arm meets opposite leg.

Hard: Hold weights in the hands. Keep arms (straight) still and focus instead on keeping the shoulder blades down and together.

PULL-DOWN WITH RESISTANCE BAND (BACK MUSCLES)

Safely attach (higher than your height) a resistance band to a machine or something sturdy. Grab the resistance band with your left hand and take a step forward with your right leg *(a)*. Adjust your position so the band is taut, while the left hand stays at navel height. Lean slightly forward as one unit and keep the left heel off the floor. As always, initiate the movement with the core. Exhale and pull the resistance band down (keep the elbows soft) past the left hip. Simultaneously step forward with your left leg *(b)*. Pause in this new position and make sure the right arm is in a "handshake" position. To mimic the Nordic walking technique, keep the right hand closed in the front but open in the back. Inhale and return with control. Repeat 10 to 15 times then change sides.

Make sure you bring the hand all the way to the hip, preferably past the hip with a straight elbow. If that is not possible, decrease the weight (resistance).

Easy: Stand with both feet parallel. Use only arm movement, not leg movement.

Moderate: The moderate version is the version described in the previous paragraph and shown in the photo.

Hard: Stand on one leg. Start with the non-supporting leg in a high knee position. As you pull the opposite arm down with resistance, lower the non-supporting leg without touching the floor. Move the opposite arm in opposite direction to get a nice rhythm.

Alternative suggestions: At the gym, try a lat pull-down cable machine. At home, use a resistance band or a sport cord. The best sport cords are those that can be attached to a doorjamb. Attach it high up on the door and it will work similarly to the cable. The difference is that the weight of the cable remains the same throughout the whole range of motion. The band will provide more resistance as you pull it toward you.

SQUAT WITH CALF RAISE (LEG AND CALF MUSCLES)

Place feet hip-width apart. Inhale and squat down *(a)*. Lead with the buttocks. Make sure the knees stay behind the toes. Exhale and return past the starting position, finishing with a calf raise *(b)*. Repeat 10 to 15 times.

Go only as far down as the knee and feet allow. Keep good alignment; otherwise pull back on the depth of the squat.

Easy: Skip the calf raise segment.

Moderate: Hold the squat position for three counts before returning.

Hard: Add a jump after the calf raise.

KICKBACK (TRICEPS MUSCLES)

Hold a weight in each hand. Place feet hip-width apart. Slightly bend the knees and bend the hips, keeping your back straight and parallel to the floor *(a)*. Shoulder blades are back and down and the neck is aligned with the spine. Raise elbows so that they're parallel with the back. Exhale and straighten the elbows, pause, and return in a controlled manner *(b)*. Repeat 10 to 15 times.

There should be absolutely no strain on the lower back. Keep core and buttocks activated to protect the lower back.

Easy: The back and the working arm are in the same position, but place the nonworking hand and same leg on a bench for support. The other leg is on the floor next to the bench and slightly soft.

Moderate: The moderate version is the version described in the previous paragraph and shown in the photo.

Hard: Stand on one leg.

HANDSHAKE (BICEPS AND SHOULDER MUSCLES)

Place feet hip-width apart. Hold hand weights at your sides (palms facing the thighs) and focus on keeping the shoulder blades activated (down and together). Move the arm up to a handshake position (elbow slightly bent) and end at the height of your navel *(a)*. Alternate arms and move in a controlled manner *(b)*.

Focus on keeping the shoulder blades activated throughout the range of motion.

Easy: Same as the photo and description in previous paragraph.

Moderate: Start with feet hip-width apart. Step out into a lunge as the opposite arm lifts up into the handshake position. Return to starting position. Repeat 10 to 15 times on each side.

Hard: Stand on one leg.

LEANING CORE (SHOULDERS AND CORE MUSCLES)

Kneel down on a mat or something soft in front of a stability ball. Place the hands on the ball *(a)*. Keep a good form. Inhale and lean forward (as one unit) on the stability ball *(b)*. Exhale and return as one unit. Repeat 10 to 15 times. Move only as far forward as core strength allows. If the buttocks is left behind, return and start over with only an inch of leaning forward.

There should be absolutely no strain on the lower back. Keep core and buttocks activated to protect the lower back.

Easy: Lean against something sturdy instead of the stability ball. Hold the position instead of moving back and forth.

Moderate: Pause in the leaning position and hold it for three or more counts and then return.

Hard: Choose a smaller stability ball. Roll out until the elbows touch the ball.

SHOULDER BLADE SQUEEZE (BACK MUSCLES)

Kneel down with the feet touching a wall behind you for support. Pull a stability ball as close to you as possible. As you lean on it with the front of your body, facing down, straighten the legs as you roll out, away from the wall *(a)*. From the side, you should look like one straight line (almost parallel to the floor) from the feet to the head. Your feet are supported by the wall. Your legs are active and straight, your belly is on the ball but the core is active, and your arms are by your side with the palms

facing down but active shoulder blades. As you roll out into this position, it may be easier to keep the hands on the floor to maintain the balance. Review the points about good form. Every muscle in your body should be activated. Squeeze the shoulder blades and slowly lift the arms up and down in a small range of motion *(b)*. Initiate the arm movement every time from the shoulder blades. Now, add weights to your hands and get into the same position. Keep the range of motion small and pause each time in the end position to increase the awareness of the squeezing of the shoulder blades. Perform the movement 10 to 15 times. Focus on squeezing the shoulder blades and opening the chest.

There should be absolutely no strain on the lower back. Keep the core and buttocks activated to protect the lower back.

Easy: Use no weights or movement. Stay in this position as long as you can.

Moderate: The moderate version is the version described in the previous paragraph and shown in the photo.

Hard: Do the exercise with no support from the wall. Only one leg is on the floor.

Endurance Training for Nordic Walking

The training recommended for Nordic walking is endurance for your muscles as well as your heart, blood vessels, and lungs (cardiorespiratory system). Endurance means the ability to maintain something for a prolonged time. In muscular endurance training, it involves improving your ability to lift a weight for 15 times before your muscles fatigue. In cardiorespiratory endurance (aerobic), it involves improving your ability to maintain an exercise that involves large muscle groups for more than five minutes nonstop. Examples of such aerobic exercises are walking, running, biking, swimming, and cross-country skiing.

The actual recommendation for improving aerobic capacity is 20 to 60 minutes of cardiorespiratory activity, three to five days a week, at a moderate to hard intensity. Chapter 7 contains a practical example of a typical Nordic walking workout based on those recommendations.

Why Do You Need Aerobic Training?

It is not enough to *say* that it is good for you. Instead ask what makes it good for you. Humans cannot live without oxygen. When oxygen is breathed in through the lungs, it is transferred (exchange of gases) into the bloodstream. The heart pumps the blood around in the body and thus the blood can continue to transport the oxygen farther to the active cells. If a muscle is at rest, it may be content with the energy that is stored in the body and thus no extra oxygen is needed for energy production. However, the storage will run out after you start running for a few minutes. The active muscles will now need more oxygen to produce energy to sustain the activity for more than three minutes. The better your cardiorespiratory system can deliver and use oxygen, the better aerobic shape you are in. If you climb the stairs of the Empire State Building in New York, you might be able to climb only a few flights with no previous aerobic training. Your heart, blood vessels, and lungs are not accustomed to this high demand. If you are consistent with your aerobic training, you can come back after two weeks and see that you no longer are out of breath after a couple of floors. Eventually you may even be able to climb all 86 floors.

Most, if not all, sports require an endurance phase in the yearly training program, and it is then regarded as your base. Once you have your base established, you branch off into other sport-specific training phases. For a sprinter competing in a 100-meter dash, training involves a lot of speed training (shorter distances plus faster speed). Although a marathon runner will include some speed workouts at some point in an annual training plan, the overall goal remains endurance (longer distances plus slower speed).

There are various ways to increase your aerobic capacity. And just as the strength training section advised you to vary your workouts to avoid plateaus, the same principle applies to endurance training. The three ways used in the Nordic walking workout in part II are continuous training, interval training, and hill training.

COMMON BENEFITS OF ENDURANCE SPORTS AND ACTIVITIES

- Increased aerobic capacity
- Reduced risk of cardiovascular diseases (heart attack, stroke)
- Reduced risk of type 2 diabetes
- Improved stamina
- Less fatigue
- Ease in doing daily activities
- Improved resting blood pressure
- Decreased total cholesterol
- Increased HDL (good cholesterol)
- Decreased body fat

Continuous Training

This is the most common method of aerobic training. You perform the aerobic activity at the same intensity (excluding warming up and cooling down gradually) nonstop. It can get boring, so sometimes it helps to spice it up with the other two types of endurance training. However, it is great for beginners who want to gradually improve aerobic capacity. Starting out with high-intensity interval training can be intimidating as well as discouraging. Ease into the continuous training and enjoy it at the level that feels comfortable. Build the base and then get creative and mix it up.

Interval Training

Aerobic interval training consists of short, high-intensity bouts that you repeat over and over. You get to rest in between each bout, though it's a brief rest. This way the aerobic system stays stressed because you never get to recover fully. The aerobic benefit seems to be the same whether you do continuous training at a high intensity or interval training. However, the variation of the intervals makes it more fun. Usually the intervals can last from 15 seconds to 5 minutes. It is easier to start out with longer intervals and keep a good pace instead of sprinting full out for 10 seconds at a time. If you were a sprinter, you would work toward the shorter bouts.

The shortest intervals used in the Nordic walking workouts in this book are 60 seconds. The rest period does not always have to mean that you stop but that you slow down the pace to light or moderate—enough for you to feel somewhat recovered before you start another interval. Another way of doing intervals is to keep the interval as long as the resting period. For example, do 3 minutes at a moderate to high intensity and then recover for 3 minutes at a light intensity. Another way is to do 5 minutes at a fast pace and then 2 1/2 minutes at a light pace. There are endless ways to do intervals, and maybe you will find a combination that works great for you so you'll keep going. The main thing, unless you are a competitive athlete, is to vary the speed and make it fun.

Hill Training

If you have ever followed the Tour de France race, you know what hill training can do to you. It is a great endurance training tool that provides a fun variation. Depending on the degree of incline and distance, it can take the intensity up a good notch. If you live in an area with hills, take advantage of them. Hills can also serve as a way of tracking your progress. Maybe the first time you will not be able to reach the top. But the day you do, you know that you have made progress. You can also time yourself and see how fast you can go up the hill. Sometimes you find one perfect hill and you can use that one for a good portion of your day's workout: Going uphill will be the high-intensity portion; going downhill will be the rest period. It becomes a form of interval training.

Cross-Training

Even though you will fall in love with Nordic walking and practice it several times a week, a time will come when you may want to try something else temporarily. You don't stop Nordic walking; you just mix it up with another endurance activity. Don't worry—it happens in any sport or exercise. Actually, it is recommended to vary physical activities for several reasons. If the body does the same thing year in and year out, it will get very good at that one thing. When the body becomes efficient, it burns fewer calories. As you will see in part II, you can vary a Nordic walking workout to prevent this from happening and you can cross-train. Cross-training is a good way to avoid overusing certain muscles and joints, which will prevent injuries. If you already have an injury, there is no question about the benefit of stopping what you are doing and shifting activities for a while. You can also become injured from overtraining. It is a good thing to vary the training and the activities to give the injured body part a chance to heal. Contact a health and fitness professional, who can design a balanced program. Also remember to take at least one day off a week to rest. Resting allows the body to recover and to become stronger.

Instead of totally changing activities, you can cross-train by dividing the week up with a variety of activities. Instead of Nordic walking five times a week, cut it down to three times a week; on the other two days, try other aerobic activities. Following is a list of aerobic activities that you can use in cross-training. You will still achieve aerobic benefits because the activities use large muscle groups with a dynamic and continuous rhythm.

CROSS-TRAINING ENDURANCE SPORTS AND ACTIVITIES

- Jogging and running
- Biking
- Swimming
- Nordic blading (see photo on page 16)
- Nordic fitness skiing and cross-country skiing (see photo on page 17)
- Nordic snowshoeing (see photo on page 17)
- Nordic winter walking (see photo on page 17)

If you are looking for wintertime activities to complement Nordic walking, try Nordic winter walking, Nordic snowshoeing, and classic-style Nordic skiing. Variations are Nordic blading during the dry seasons and skating-style Nordic skiing in the winter. The latter two have the skating aspect in common. The main goal is that you find activities that you enjoy. Cross-training activities motivate you to stay in shape year-round and present less risk of injury.

Conclusion

It is very easy to do things you are good at and to avoid working on your weaknesses. In business, your advice would be to hire the people who excel and thrive at the things you resist doing. The best advice in physical fitness is to aim for a balanced body. This means you need to work on aspects of the body that are weak or inexperienced. Maybe you need more strength training to keep the muscles and bones working for a long time. Maybe you need to improve your flexibility in order to avoid aches and pain in the future. Maybe you need to make your heart stronger by doing more endurance training. After this chapter, you should feel equipped to train all of these aspects of fitness as well as use these aspects in preparing for Nordic walking. Remember to change your workouts. Avoid doing the same thing day in and day out. The body strives for balance to make things easier. Once it gets good at something, it will take less of an effort to do it. That means the body will burn fewer calories. So keep challenging the body to train for life and all its endeavors. Variation is the key to a balanced body.

CHAPTER 3

Poles, Footwear, and Clothing

Impatience never commanded success.

Edwin H. Chapin

Would you hit a tennis ball with a badminton racket? No. As with any other sport, Nordic walking requires specific equipment so that you can perform the movements as efficiently as possible. Nordic walking poles are planted behind the body at an angle and have angled spike tips and paws. Trekking poles need to have straight spike tips to provide balance and support when planted in a vertical position in front of the body. The straps of Nordic walking poles need to fit snugly, supporting the hand as you push the pole back and away from the body. Downhill ski poles have straps with simple loops because the hand never leaves the grip, and the points in the poles are for initiating turns. So just don't grab your ski poles to go Nordic walking. The Nordic walking poles are designed to fit the specific needs and purposes of Nordic walking. As the sport continues to develop and becomes more sophisticated through further research, the pole companies have to make adjustments accordingly. The same requirements apply to Nordic walking footwear, clothing, and accessories.

After reading this chapter, you will be able to choose appropriate clothing from head to toe as well as equipment for Nordic walking. Additionally, you will understand how helpful a heart rate monitor is and you'll ask yourself how you could have lived without one all these years. The accessories will make your workouts much more enjoyable. In general, the poles are low maintenance, but there are some simple guidelines on caring for them so that the poles as well as their various parts last for a long time.

The adjustability of trekking poles makes them heavier and might provide too much vibration for the continuous rhythm of Nordic walking. The key in Nordic walking is to enhance walking and keep the poles as light as possible to maintain a natural walking pattern. A trekking pole can be used on narrow, rugged, and slanted trails. Adjusting one side to be shorter and the other to be longer provides support and balance. The planting motion is usually in a vertical position, thus the straight spike tip. The planting in Nordic walking is at an angle that is maintained throughout the movement, and sometimes you will find an angled spike tip to boost the traction. There is no use for an asphalt paw since the trekking trails mainly require traction from a spike tip. The asphalt paw in Nordic walking allows you to get a workout on the sidewalks in the city as well. Similarly, there is no use for a snug and adjustable strap in trekking since the movement does not require a large range of motion. A simple loop strap is enough while trekking. A snug and comfortable strap that acts as a cradle for the hand is essential in Nordic walking for transferring the power and staying connected to the pole in advanced techniques. People who trek need support and balance. People who Nordic walk look to get the best workout without interruption. Two different purposes bring about two differently made poles.

Selecting Nordic Walking Poles

All good Nordic walking poles have a few features in common, but the choice of features becomes a matter of personal preference. I prefer a lightweight pole that has very little vibration, a comfortable and ergonomic grip, and straps that are easy to get into and stay in place so I don't have to constantly readjust (see figures 3.1 and 3.2). I also like to feel that the strap remains part of the hand in a release of the grip in more advanced Nordic walking techniques. I prefer a strapless pole when I work with the elderly population because most elderly people do only the basic Nordic walking technique or a modified version of it (see figure 3.3). I like an angled spike tip for great traction on dirt and an asphalt paw that has a big surface area for push-off and has great cushioning when planted on asphalt. For everyday use at home, I prefer either a one-length pole or an extensible one (see figure 3.4). For traveling, I prefer an adjustable pole (see figure 3.5). The main difference between adjustable and extensible poles is the location of the adjustment. On the adjustable pole, it takes place in

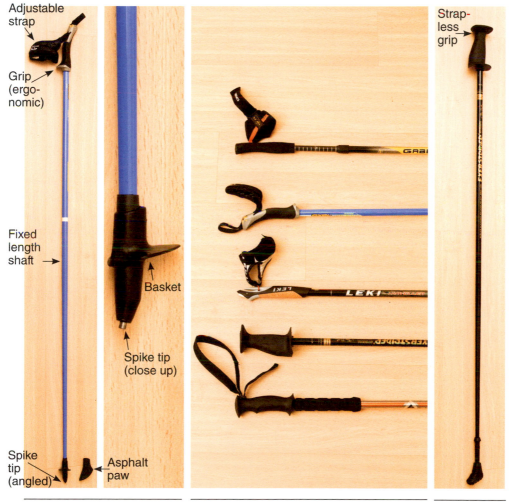

Figure 3.1 A one-length pole showing common features of a Nordic walking pole.

Figure 3.2 Various straps and grips.

Figure 3.3 Strapless pole.

the middle of the pole. On the extensible one, it occurs at the top of the pole, making it less prone to vibration of the shaft. When I do demonstrations with a large group, it's easier to deal with adjustable or extensible ones if I were to run out of a certain size of pole. Sometimes a person can be in between two heights of poles; adjustable or extensible poles alleviate that problem. A fixed (one-length) pole is ideal for the elderly population to avoid having to rely on the adjustment mechanism working properly. The following is a list of features of the various types of poles. Table 3.1 is a comparison chart detailing the types of poles, and figures 3.1 to 3.6 show a variety of poles. As always, your personal preferences will determine what type of pole fits your needs.

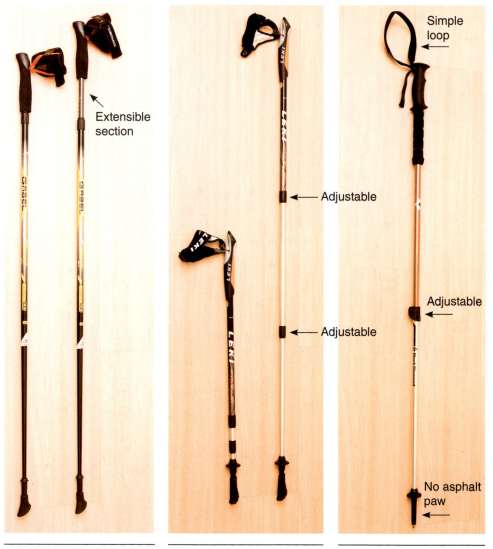

Figure 3.4 Extensible pole.

Figure 3.5 Adjustable pole collapsed for traveling and regular size for Nordic walking.

Figure 3.6 Trekking pole. This pole is made for trekking and not Nordic walking.

Table 3.1 Comparison Chart of Fixed, Extensible, and Adjustable Poles

Comment	Type of pole		
	Fixed	Extensible	Adjustable
Adjustable mechanism makes the pole heavier		X	X
Adjustment needed before each walk		X	X
Needs to be folded after each walk to maintain adjusting mechanism		X	X
Easily stowed in carry-on luggage on flights			X
Needs special bag for travel on flights	X	X	
Needs to be checked in on flights	X	X	
Easily grab and go without adjustments pre- or postwalk	X		
Adjusts to any height			X
Adjusts to fit some other heights		X	
No weak links	X		
More vibration		X	X

Keep these six factors in mind while shopping for Nordic walking poles:

1. Length
2. Straps
3. Grips
4. Shaft
5. Spike tip
6. Asphalt paw

Length

As mentioned earlier, cross-country ski poles are too tall for Nordic walking. The initial way to choose the correct size of Nordic walking poles is to check the estimated pole size based on your height (see table 3.2). When measuring your height, make sure you are standing on an even surface, and wear the shoes you'll be wearing when Nordic walking. Keep the pole in an upright (vertical) position with the tip on the ground. Hold on to the grip of the pole where the strap inserts. Keep your elbow glued to your waist. If your arm is at a 90-degree angle or slightly greater, then the pole is a good height for you (see figure 3.7).

Table 3.2 Choosing a Pole Height Based on Your Height

Find your height	Try this pole size
4'9 – 4'11 (145-150 cm)	100 cm
4'11 – 5'3 (150-160 cm)	105 cm
5'3 – 5'5 (160-165 cm)	110 cm
5'5 – 5'9 (165-175 cm)	115 cm
5'9 – 5'11 (175-180 cm)	120 cm
5'11 – 6'1 (180-185 cm)	125 cm
6'1 – 6'3 (185-190 cm)	130 cm
6'3 – 6'5 (190-196 cm)	135 cm

If you purchase poles online, there should be correct pole size charts you can view as you enter your own height. If you purchase in stores, the staff should be able to find the correct size for you.

The question of whether to purchase one-length (fixed-length) or adjustable poles is a matter of personal choice. Table 3.1 will help you answer the questions you may have before you make your decision. Prices vary from year to year, but price is always a factor to consider when you purchase a product. Appendix A contains a resource guide to various brands of Nordic walking poles. You should be able to find the current price on the pole you are interested in. Some companies specialize in either one-length or adjustable poles, but usually they carry both choices.

If you do purchase adjustable poles, make sure you get proper instruction on adjusting them. Instructions vary from year to year and brand to brand, and this book does not provide instructions for all types of poles. Purchases online usually include an instructional DVD. In a retail store the staff should be able to help you. Class instructors who sell poles should also be experts on the brands of poles they are selling.

Straps

Sorry, your downhill ski poles won't work since they have a different type of strap with a simple loop, which

Figure 3.7 Correct height of pole for this person.

CONSUMER TIP

Make sure you purchase poles that fit you. Check the chart for your height and corresponding size of the poles.

is also used on trekking poles. The simple loop is sufficient in downhill skiing and trekking pursuits because you always hold the grip in the palm of your hand. Those straps do not allow you to extend back and reach a full range of motion; cross-country skiing and Nordic walking pole straps do allow those movements. The Nordic walking pole strap gives the hand maximal support in the transfer of the power from the planting phase through the pushing back phase of the pole. When you release the hand at the end of the push-back phase (for the more advanced Nordic walking technique), the pole becomes one with the arm via the strap. In other words, the pole becomes an extension of your arm. A cross-country skier performs the same extended movement as a Nordic walker, which is why the straps are similar. For this reason, it is important for the strap to be adjustable. Hands come in various sizes. It should be a snug fit. You need to be able to adjust the strap so it fits *your* hand perfectly. If the strap is too loose, you will not have control over the pole as you release the handgrip behind you. When the strap is adjusted correctly, it provides support for the hand, which allows you to hold on *lightly* to the grip of the pole. As you will learn in part II, you need to be able to create tension in the muscles but also be able to relax them. A snug fit will be necessary when you soften the grip at the end of the push-back phase at any level. The strap is then able to transfer the power.

Some poles are strapless; this feature solves the mystery of strapping in and out. It is very convenient to just grab the poles and go. However, you will not be able to perform the more advanced Nordic walking techniques completely as mentioned previously. Another advantage with straps is that you don't have to rely on holding on to the grip of the pole; the strap gives your hand enough support. Sometimes people hold on to the grip for dear life instead of relying on

SAFETY TIP

Be careful in handling the poles while adjusting the straps and removing and adding paws. Once you remove the asphalt paw, the spike tip is exposed and it can be sharp. Always keep the spike tips pointing down toward the ground when not Nordic walking. This is easy to forget while adjusting things on the poles. Make sure you have lots of free space around you.

the support of the strap. This is something to keep in mind if you have arthritis and have a hard time getting a grip. If you have high blood pressure, it is also good to keep a light grip. (Whenever you tighten the muscles, not only does it create tension in the muscles, but it also increases the tension on the blood vessels, which causes constriction.) Absolutely no white knuckles! A light grip can be achieved with strapless poles; you just have to be more aware of it. Strapless poles are ideal for the elderly population because they're not likely to be set on doing any advanced Nordic walking techniques. The basic Nordic walking technique (see chapter 6) involves simply pushing the hand to the hip. It is not necessary to strap in with the basic technique. Learning Nordic walking is easier for the elderly if they don't have to learn the extra step of strapping in. Elderly people tend to feel more comfortable when not strapped in because if a fall were to happen, it is easier to let go of the pole grip than to feel trapped while strapped in.

There are straps that are quite easy to get in and out of. They can be just plugged in or out of the pole so that you don't have to worry about how to get in and out of the strap. Strapping in can be harder than learning how to Nordic walk. These types of poles have only two disadvantages: They may not give you enough of a solid, snug feeling while applying the advanced technique; and there is a weak link at the top of the pole. Make sure you always keep them plugged in when you don't use them so you don't lose the strap.

Of all exercises walking is the best.

Thomas Jefferson

Whether you purchase poles with attached straps, with plug-in-straps, or without straps, make sure you get proper instruction on using them. As mentioned earlier, instructions vary from year to year and brand to brand, so this book does not cover instructions for all of them. Above all, make sure your hands and fingers are comfortable. A pair of thin gloves can provide more comfort and keep your hands warm during cold seasons.

Grips

Choices, choices, choices. You probably never thought there would be so many things to consider when buying two sticks. This section covers only a few features to make the choice easier. The strap is connected to the grip. As stated earlier, manufacturers are constantly developing new and enhanced features, so the best way to keep up to date on equipment is to visit the Web sites listed in appendix A. When I first started out in 2002, the pole grip was straight and the material was rubber. Today you will still find straight grips but also grips that have more of a bent and form-fitted shape to provide a more ergonomic position for the hand, which makes it more comfortable. More comfort is not a hard choice, but on top of that the grips are made out of various materials (rubber, plastic, or cork) and there may even be more to choose from after this book is published. All of these special features are a very personal choice. For example, cork is supposed to be a warmer material, which makes it nice for those cold winter days. Unfortunately, a certain material might be available only in straight grips. The question is whether to choose comfort for the hands all year-round or mainly in the cold season.

Shaft

Nordic walking is an enhancement of regular walking. The whole pole should be lightweight so that you can maintain a natural arm swing. Mainly the material of the shaft will determine its weight. Most common materials are carbon fiber and aluminum. Some poles are made of a combination of the two materials. Carbon fiber is very light and so is aluminum, but aluminum creates more vibration. Both materials are durable and flexible, though carbon fiber

CONSUMER TIP

See figure 3.6 to review the main features that make the trekking pole different from a Nordic walking pole. The heaviness or the material of a trekking pole cannot be seen in the photo. Remember, the lighter the pole, the more natural arm swing and more natural walking pattern can be maintained. The material of a trekking pole will most likely result in too much vibration.

glass can break more easily. Make sure you get a lifetime guarantee on those shafts. If a pole vibrates too much, the vibration will be absorbed by the body instead of by the pole. If you have any upper-body injuries, you want the pole to absorb the vibration as much as possible. One-length, semi-extensible, and adjustable poles are available. The fixed length requires you only to change your body position while going up or down hill. The semi-extensible ones give you more freedom in changing the height of the pole. The adjustable pole allows you to change the height to fit almost anyone. This feature also makes it great for traveling since it most likely can be collapsed to fit in your suitcase. The downside is that it makes it heavier because of the added mechanism that adjusts the pole.

Spike Tip

A lot of people think they have seen people Nordic walking when they actually have seen them trekking instead in the mountains. One of the differences between a trekking pole and a Nordic walking pole is the spike tip. The tip is vertical on a trekking pole because you need to place the pole in front of you in a vertical position to get support. The spike tip on a Nordic walking pole is angled to provide a better grip when placing the pole in an angled position. However, you'll find many good Nordic walking poles with a straight spike tip. Don't let this feature—angled or straight spike tip—be the decisive factor in choosing a pole. As mentioned, the main differences between trekking and Nordic walking lie in the use of the pole (vertical compared to angled pole plant) and the technique (keeping the pole in front of your body the whole time compared to pushing it back behind your body at the end).

Asphalt Paw

The great thing about Nordic walking is that you can do it on any surface. You can basically start from your doorstep and go Nordic walking down the sidewalk, into the park on the grass, across the dirt track, and right out onto the sandy beach. No need to get into your car to travel to go exercising. This versatility of Nordic walking is made possible with one tiny addition: the asphalt paw (see

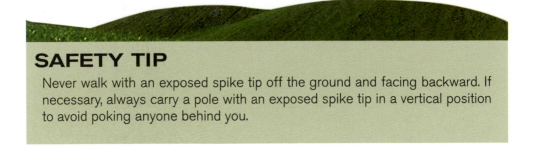

SAFETY TIP

Never walk with an exposed spike tip off the ground and facing backward. If necessary, always carry a pole with an exposed spike tip in a vertical position to avoid poking anyone behind you.

figure 3.8). It looks like a little shoe for the pole. By covering the spike tip with an asphalt paw, you can walk on asphalt and concrete. By removing the paw, you can use the spike tip on grass, dirt, and icy surfaces. If you are a beginner, you can keep the paw on when walking in sand. If you're more advanced, take the paw off while walking in sand—it proves much more difficult since the whole pole sinks down deeper in the sand without the paw.

Figure 3.8 The asphalt paw makes Nordic walking versatile.

Some poles have a basket at the end of the pole. As you place the paw back on, make sure you line up the paw so that it points in the same direction as the basket. If your pole is "basket free," then usually the instructions on the DVD tell you how to line it up correctly. No matter what poles you use, the general rule is that the "toe" of the paw points backward. Because of the form of the paw, it offers the best traction in this position. Asphalt paws come in various shapes and sizes; some have bigger surface areas to provide better traction, some have a spike tip poking through to supply a better grip, and some are shaped like a bell for better balance. Some paws come with dubs like your car tires use in the winter time. It provides better traction not only for the winter, but on wet surfaces and in general. There is now also an asphalt paw and a spike tip that come as one attachment—like a 2-for-1 deal. It is placed at the end of the pole and when you don't use the paw, you only kick it back to expose the spike tip.

Another amazing feature of this tiny paw is that it acts as a cushion that makes less of an impact on your upper-body joints as you walk on the harder surfaces. Asphalt paws do wear out, so purchase two pairs upfront. If you hear a click when planting the pole on asphalt, even with the paw on, it is time to

SAFETY TIP

When you remove the asphalt paw from the pole, you expose the spike tip. Be cautious and aware of your surroundings.

change paws. Another sign is when you feel you don't get great traction any-more on asphalt surfaces. To keep the paws lasting as long as possible, keep changing surfaces. This is great both for your Nordic walking technique *and* for your wallet.

Selecting Nordic Walking Shoes

Some shoe companies produce shoes specifically for Nordic walking, whereas others produce regular walking shoes that can be used for Nordic walking. Most of the types of shoe can best be described as a cross-breed shoe for walking and trail running. Some of them have a very low sole to promote what is called dorsiflexion. This is a correct way of walking—landing with the heel first. A few shoe companies think like the Norse and focus on weather-resistant materials. Since the interest in Nordic walking has increased so dramatically, more specifically designed Nordic walking shoes keep entering the market. Appendix A is a resource guide for various brands of Nordic walking shoes.

All good Nordic walking shoes have a few features in common, but after that it becomes a very personal choice. I prefer a shoe that is light and form fitted so that it feels like part of my foot. The shoes should provide great traction so that I can use them for Nordic hiking on dirt as well as on asphalt. It's a plus if the shoes are made with water-resistant material. Since the footwork in regular walking is the same as in Nordic walking, the shoes must have the features of great walking shoes: a flexible front for great push-off, support under the mid-foot, and a rounded heel to promote dorsiflexion (see figure 3.9).

Regular walking and Nordic walking are very similar in terms of the type of wear and tear on your foot as well as on your shoe. In both, you land with the most pressure on the center of the heel. Then you roll onto the foot with first a slight weight shift to the outside of the foot (supination) and then toward the inside of the foot (pronation). As you roll onto the ball of the foot, the heel gradually lifts off the ground to prepare for the push with the ball of the

Figure 3.9   The shoe *(a)* needs to have a rounded heel to provide a good heel strike when landing, *(b)* needs to provide good support as you put all your weight on that foot, and *(c)* it needs to bend in the front to provide a good push-off.

foot. Executing the whole movement properly (landing with the heel to push off with the toes; see figure 3.10) requires enough flexibility in the joints of the foot and enough muscle strength in the buttocks to prevent the foot from excess pronation (arch collapse). Shoe makers are aware of these common weaknesses and thus focus on creating shoes that will support these weak areas. Any movement you do over a long period needs to be done in as much of a correct fashion as possible to avoid unnecessary wear and tear on the joints. Chapter 6 explores the basics of regular walking, including increasing your awareness of how you work the feet as you walk.

Unless you purchase the shoe online, pick it up and test it. Can it bend in the front? If so, good. Move on to the middle of the shoe. Make sure the middle does not bend too much. That's where you need some support. Finally, check out the heel of the shoe. Is it somewhat rounded? If it's too hard to tell, compare it with the heel of a running shoe. The impact of a runner's heel in the landing phase is much greater than a walker's. A shoe's heel needs more cushion for a runner and less cushion for a walker. Make sure you can walk around with a good roll-through motion. There should be no sound of the forefoot slamming the ground. It can cause pain in the shin or even shin splints. Just as a good pair of Nordic walking poles helps you maintain the natural rhythm of walking, good Nordic walking shoes should do the same. Forget sandals only because of the risk of planting the spike tip on your foot instead of on the ground.

The fact that you can take Nordic walking anywhere and on almost any surface will make the purchasing of the shoe even more important. I like the fact that the Nordic walking shoes that have been customized to the sport have some trail features to them. If you have ever been hiking, you know that regular walking shoes often slip on rocky surfaces. The same is true of icy

Figure 3.10 Proper movement of the feet.

CONSUMER TIP

Do you purchase products without reading the instructions? Learning how to use the poles properly is essential for gaining all the promised benefits. At least learn the basics (see chapter 6). It will take you 5 to 15 minutes.

and snowy surfaces. Check the sole of the shoe. It should be ribbed to provide great traction.

When purchasing your Nordic walking shoes, ask for weather-resistant materials. Think of the Scandinavian weather conditions: People year-round in snow, slush, ice, and wind. The clothes and shoes will be made with the most extreme weather in mind. Rainy and snowy conditions can never stop you from Nordic walking if you are dressed properly.

Providing enough room for your toes in the shoes is another important comfort factor. Different shoes come in different sizes. European sizes have even a tendency to vary a lot between brands. Take this into account when purchasing online. Sometimes shoe companies will say whether the sizes match regular shoe sizes. If they run smaller than your regular shoes, purchase them in one size larger than your regular shoe size.

Purchase a good pair of Nordic walking shoes because you want to keep the feet happy. Some of the shoes featured in appendix A may work best as a training shoe to encourage correct gait (walking technique). As you get into tougher workouts requiring more agility, those shoes might be too heavy or even somewhat clumsy. Every shoe has its place and purpose, and determining your best brand of shoe is a very personal choice.

Selecting the Right Socks

Don't forget to get some good socks. Avoid cotton socks whether it is summer or winter because they absorb too much moisture. The shoe is the outer layer for the foot and the moisture gets trapped. Wool manages moisture well, but it is too itchy for most feet, unless you can find merino or worsted wool. Still too itchy? Try polyester or nylon. While those materials do not get rid of the moisture, the manufacturers apply a coating that will. Check out Coolmax and Ultimax brands of socks. Or try acrylic materials, like a Thorlo sock.

Dressing for the Outdoors

As with cross-country skiing, it is best to dress in layers for Nordic walking. Because your upper body is engaged, it is amazing how fast those layers will get peeled off, even in chilly weather. In general, think light, thin, and comfortable. You want clothing that you can easily move around in—nothing binding, constricting, or chaffing. Don't forget that useful vest—it will keep the vital organs warm and protected.

The reason for dressing in layers is to maintain normal body temperature by avoiding either getting too hot or getting too cold. Each layer has a purpose and, as you will see, may not be necessary for every type of weather. The first layer is the closest to the skin; it removes the moisture to either keep the body warm or keep it cool. Cotton is fine for warm weather, but avoid using it as you add other layers for colder weather. Use silk instead. A synthetic material such as polyester also provides good ventilation. If a second layer is needed as an insulating layer, a great material is fleece. There is a variety of thicknesses of fleece, and it usually is measured in numbers (100 to 300) or in weight (light to heavy). A higher number means it is warmer but may also be too bulky. The third layer is the one that will protect you from wind and water. The best known material for water resistance is Gore-Tex. Make sure this layer is also breathable to let the heat escape. Find a somewhat form-fitted jacket so that you can move the arms freely and comfortably.

During cold weather, you need a head cover to keep the body heat from escaping. If it's sunny and warm, you want a head cover to protect you from the rays of the sun. As you leave the house and start Nordic walking you may have forgotten that hat. Table 3.3 is a checklist to keep handy before heading out. Remember that these choices are only suggestions. What is warm to one person may be cold to you. The bottom line is to dress for the weather to keep *you* warm or cool and comfortable.

Choosing Accessories

As the sport of Nordic walking grows, more products will enter the market to aid in your technique and efficiency. For example, there have been many versions of the plug, which keeps some strap mechanisms in place. Similarly there have been many versions of straps that are easily plugged into the grip of the pole. Only one of the accessories listed in this section is used specifically for Nordic walking: the snow basket. The other two can be used for any other aerobic exercises.

Heart Rate Monitor

A heart rate monitor measures how fast or slow your heart beats per minute. It comes with two units: a belt and a watch (see figure 3.11). The belt is worn around the chest, and it transmits the beats to a monitor that you wear just like a regular watch on your wrist. You will be able to read your heart rate (pulse) from the watch.

A heart rate monitor ensures that you work out at a safe zone for your heart. No need to stop to check the pulse anymore. Now you only need to look down

Table 3.3   Clothing and Accessory Suggestions Based on Weather Conditions

Choices of clothing and accessories	Weather condition
First layer is for ventilation; avoid cotton unless it is the only layer	
Second layer is for insulation; try fleece	
Third layer is for protection; try Gore-Tex	
Head	
Sun hat	Warm and sunny
Hat, hood, scarf	Cool and slightly windy
	Cold or cold and windy
Upper body	
Tank top or T-shirt or thin and light-colored long-sleeved shirt	Warm and sunny
Warm and thin long-sleeved shirt plus a light and thin vest	Cool and slightly windy
Warm and thin long-sleeved shirt plus thin fleece plus warm and thin vest	Cold
Warm and thin long-sleeved shirt plus thicker fleece plus light windbreaker	Cold and windy
Lower body	
Shorts or light and thin full-length or knee-length tights or light sweatpants	Warm and sunny
Light and thin full-length tights or light sweatpants	Cool and slightly windy
Warm and thin full-length tights or sweatpants	Cold
Warm and thin full-length tights plus light windbreaker pants	Cold and windy
Hands	
Light and thin gloves	Cool and slightly windy
Warmer gloves if your hands get cold easily	Cold or cold and windy
Accessories	
Water belt with a pocket for asphalt paws	All weather conditions
Sunscreen, sunglasses	Warm and sunny

*For rainy or snowy conditions, add Gore-Tex or similar fabric for upper and lower body.

as if you were checking your watch, but instead you check the number that measures your heart rate at that exact moment. Other features include readouts on the number of calories burned during the workout and your average heart rate so you can make sure you stay within the proper heart rate zone during the whole workout. There are many more beneficial features that you can read about in the manual included with each heart rate monitor. Some heart rate monitors are very simple to set up, whereas others may require more extensive instructions from the manual. It's a one-time setup, and it's well worth your time. Heart rate monitors require minimal mainte- nance. Use a damp cloth to clean the perspiration from the belt. Store it in a cool and dry place. If it stops work- ing, it is probably time for a battery replacement.

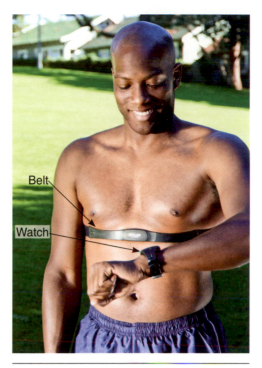

Figure 3.11 A heart rate monitor is like the speedometer of a car: It lets you know whether your body is working within a safe range.

FREQUENTLY ASKED QUESTIONS ABOUT HEART RATE MONITORS

Question: Why would I need a heart rate monitor?
Answer: To know how fast you're driving your car, you need to look at the speedom- eter. It helps you stay within the speed limits. A heart rate monitor works the same way. It will tell you how fast your heart is beating per minute.
Question: Why can't I just take the pulse?
Answer: Taking the pulse requires you to stop your exercise. If you were to stop exercising, the heartbeat would drop significantly. Stopping to check the heart rate is an inaccurate method.
Question: Who should use a heart rate monitor?
Answer: In general, anyone with a healthy heart. If you take any medications that affect your heart, the heart rate will not be accurate. Here is a list of some common medications that can affect the heart rate. We may not have added all of them, so make sure to ask your doctor as well: blood pressure medication; beta blockers; nitrates; calcium channel blockers; digitalis; vasodilators; bronchodilators; antiarrhythmic-replacement medications; antidepressants; tranquilizers; nicotine; thyroid medications; diet pills. Always check with your doctor to determine your target heart rate while exercising.

Water Belt

Whether you are exercising or not, a water belt that leaves your hands free is a great invention. It allows you to stay hydrated at all times (see figure 3.12). It is also great for traveling. Most sport stores carry water belts. Some belts have an additional pocket in the front on the belt to be used as a storage place for the asphalt paws. Try out the belt as you walk so you can make sure the bottles will not be in the way during your arm swing. A bottle placed on the belt behind you is definitely out of your way. If the pocket for the bottle is slanted, it will be easier to pull the bottle out from behind. Make sure you wash the plastic bottle to avoid bacteria buildup. Also change bottles once in a while. (There are many studies about the safety of various kinds of plastic bottles. None of those studies are discussed in this book; we are merely bringing it to your attention.)

Figure 3.12 A water belt helps you keep your hands free for the Nordic walking poles.

Snow Basket

As mentioned in chapter 1, the Nordic walking technique can apply to modified physical activities year-round. One example is snowshoeing. Add your Nordic walking poles and go Nordic snowshoeing. Although you may need to rent or purchase some snowshoes, you can definitely use the same poles. This time it is not enough to just remove the asphalt paw to change surfaces; you also need to take off the spike tip unit. Replace the spike tips with snow baskets to avoid sinking down too deep in the snow and to give you some balance (see figure 3.13). It is a small investment for the year-round use of one pair of Nordic walking poles.

Figure 3.13 Add snow baskets to your poles so you can use them for Nordic snowshoeing.

Visit the pole companies' Web sites (see appendix A) to find information on purchasing the accessories. If you purchased the poles in a store, that store may sell the accessories as well. If you bought the poles from an instructor teaching Nordic walking classes, he or she may carry a stock of other accessories or may know the best place to purchase the accessories. Ask and you will receive.

Function and Maintenance of Gear

Before you start Nordic walking, check that the asphalt paws have enough traction. As mentioned earlier, you should avoid letting them wear down so much that the spike tip starts poking through. Always purchase two pairs at a time so that you can have one readily available. The next step is to check that the paws are pointing in the correct direction. The "toes" of the paw should be pointing backward. If you have adjustable poles, now is a good time to make sure they are at a good length. Remember the 90-degree rule of the elbow (page 51). Make sure you place the right pole in your right hand and the left pole in your left hand. Sometimes it will read either *right* or *left* on the flap. Sometimes it will only be marked as R for right and L for left. As you strap in, continue checking that the strap is snug enough to give your hand full support—a feeling that the pole is part of your hand, like an extension of your arm. On most poles you can adjust the strap length as well as the tightness of the flap of the strap mechanism. If you easily get blisters, it might be a good idea to wear some thin gloves. The disadvantage is that you lose the full sensation of the squeeze and release from the grip. This is covered in more detail in part II. Another reason for blisters may be that you are strapped in incorrectly. Review the instructions from the pole company to ensure optimal comfort.

After a Nordic walking workout using the spike tips, check that the tips are free from dirt and mud before placing the paws back on. If it's not convenient to clean the tips right afterward, at least wipe them off. Then take care of the rest later at home. Let them dry before you put the paws on again. Maybe even rinse the paws while you're at it. The straps can get very wet after a sweaty workout. Wipe them off or at least let them air before you store them. If you

NORDIC WALKER TIP
Right and Left

There is a right pole and a left pole. Putting the wrong pole in the wrong hand is a common mistake. Don't worry: Often the flaps are marked to help you out.

On the contrary, there are no right and left asphalt paws. They fit on either one of the poles. No right or wrong there.

use adjustable poles, make sure you collapse them after each use to keep the adjusting mechanism functioning properly.

You can remove parts of some poles to replace them if they wear out or, for example, if you just want to try another type of grip. If you go Nordic snow-shoeing, you'll want to put on snow baskets. You can easily change paws by twisting them off. As mentioned, the grip is another part that can be replaced. Basically everything except the shaft is replaceable on some poles. Some pole companies even guarantee some shafts for a lifetime.

Conclusion

Dressing for success can be applied to sports as well. To have a successful outdoor experience, you are smart to invest into the correct equipment. Poles, shoes, and clothes should allow you to function optimally when you are Nordic walking for more than 30 minutes. Patiently consider your options with the help of the information in this chapter and from various Web sites (see appendixes A and B). If possible, join a Nordic walking class to try out different poles. To stay up to date with the Nordic walking world, you can become a member of an established Nordic walking organization (see appendix B). Most important, choose what works best for you and remember to dress both for the weather and for the activity.

CHAPTER 4

Where to Go
Nordic Walking

Sail away from the
safe harbor. Catch
the trade winds in
your sails. Explore.
Dream. Discover.

Mark Twain

Nordic walking is *the* exercise for the 21st century because it is easy, efficient, productive, and accessible. Basically, it's the most efficient full-body exercise available. You will quickly learn the basics. You will get a cardio and strength workout simultaneously. You will gain aerobic benefits faster than with regular walking. And best of all, you can start your Nordic walking workout right outside your door. No more wasting time, fuel, or money on driving to exercise. Nordic walk on sidewalks in your neighborhood, in a grassy green park, on a sandy beach to get the heart pumping, or on a trail to connect with nature. You name it, and I bet you can Nordic walk there. Not only does it work on any surface, terrain, or season, but it also works anywhere in the world—even in Antarctica.

Variation is the key to sticking to an exercise program. Nordic walking will provide not only a variety of levels of intensity but also a variety of options for location. After reading this chapter, you will have plenty of ideas of where to go Nordic walking in and around your city. You may even decide to travel to another state or country to try the specific Nordic walking routes submitted by Nordic walkers worldwide. Whether you try to find a walk in the city or on a local trail, there are some easy tips on planning the route. This book does not cover preparation for backcountry trails but recommends staying on wide and well-marked trails so you can enjoy an efficient Nordic walking workout.

Nordic Walking Anywhere

The easiest way to find an enjoyable place to Nordic walk in the city is to find a park. Think about Central Park in Manhattan. It is a sanctuary in the middle of bustling New York City. Downtown Chicago offers trails along Lake Michigan and in Millennium Park. San Francisco's Golden Gate Park has plants from almost every nation. So even if you live in a big city, you can enjoy a walk in the park as a nice getaway. In Europe, more and more Nordic fitness sports parks are popping up, which of course provide a paradise for Nordic walkers. (More information on Nordic fitness sports parks is at the end of this chapter.) Anyplace close to a mountain lends itself naturally to Nordic walking or Nordic hiking. Usually those are ideal places for people who are interested in more advanced workouts, but remember that choosing various surfaces and terrains is like choosing various levels of intensity. Maybe a 99-year-old person shouldn't Nordic walk on soft sand, but a young athlete definitely could. If a hike is too out of your way, find a challenging hilly Nordic walk in your city

NORDIC WALKER TIP

Find more Nordic walks at www.nordicwalkingusa.com. Share your favorite Nordic walk with the world.

or find a challenging surface such as soft sand. Above all, learn the more challenging techniques of Nordic walking (see chapters 8 and 9) and get the most out of those poles.

Because Nordic walking is constantly growing in popularity worldwide, hotels and spas offer special Nordic walking packages. Next time you plan a vacation, include Nordic walking and try a different form of rejuvenation—the Nordic way.

Planning the Route

The best way to find out about various Nordic walking routes is to explore your own city starting in your own neighborhood. Find some flat routes and look for those hills that will get your heart working a little bit more. Maybe there's a beautiful park in your neighborhood where you can remove the paws of the poles to enjoy Nordic walking. Always wear a watch so that you can determine the time it takes to complete a certain route for future reference. Noting your time also allows you to check your progress. If you visit another city, ask the concierge at the hotel where you can go walking. Make sure you do some research before your trip. Check out the Web site for the city or the tourist information for guided walks. Maybe you know people who have been to the city. Usually they are happy to share their favorite walks and experiences.

If you want to go Nordic hiking, you have to put a little more time into it unless you live right next to the trailhead. Visit local outdoor equipment stores. Not only do they have books on local hikes, but their staff also can recommend some real gems. They can also give you other useful information. For example, sometimes you need an adventure pass to enter and park in certain areas in the mountains. Again, if you travel, make sure you do some research ahead of time, which can include finding a local outdoor equipment retailer. Later in this chapter you will find specific examples of Nordic walking destinations worldwide. For additional information and ideas, you can visit the Web sites listed in appendix B.

Distance, Time, Elevation, and Terrain

When going for a Nordic adventure in the mountains, you need to know how long the route is and how long it will take for you individually and anyone joining you. The trails in this book are on the wide and marked trails based on

NORDIC WALKER TIP
Nordic walking offers a full-body workout from the moment you step outside your door. The days of taking time to drive to exercise are over.

an average speed of 3.5 mph (5.6 km/hr). While that may sound easy enough, there are some factors that you have to plan for. You may come to a sign that says you have only 1 mile (1.6 km) to go to get the top. On a flat and even surface, that might take no more than 15 minutes. Let's say that during the next mile you will ascend 1,000 feet (305 m). Suddenly that 1 mile may take you over an hour. If you haven't acclimatized your body, make sure you avoid elevations of more than 8,000 feet (2,438 m) above sea level. Otherwise you will have to deal with high-altitude concerns, such as shortness of breath and dizziness.

When you arrive at the trailhead, there is usually a board of information including a map of various routes in the park. Some parks may also provide maps that you can easily carry around. Choose a route. If you don't have a separate map, jot down some helpful notes, especially if there is more than one route. Focus on the intersections. The big map should also inform you about the distance and the elevation. It is amazing how much information you can get from an experienced hiker who is about to start a route. Respect that person's time, and focus your questions on time, elevation, and terrain of the route you are planning to embark on.

Always bring a watch so that you can keep track of time. If you feel good about Nordic hiking 30 minutes out, then turn around and you have completed a one-hour hike. Plan to be back way before sunset. It gets darker faster in canyons, dense forests, and mountains. Take note of the time of your start so that you are not out there for too long before you decide to turn around. If you walk in a group, make sure you always regroup at intersections. Always give yourself a mental note or, better yet, jot it down when you make a turn so you can easily backtrack in case you decide to turn around sooner.

Thoughts come clearly while one walks.

Thomas Mann

Terrain is another factor. If it's smooth and flat ground, it's easier to traverse. But if you have to climb rocks, not only will it take longer to cover the distance, but it will be harder stepping up and down on those rocks. A hilly terrain will give you a great workout, but it will also slow you down. In this book, the technique for uphill and downhill walks deals only with easy to difficult inclines but not extreme ones. Make sure you don't choose routes that are extremely steep. You don't want to have to sit down in order to slide down to safety. If it will be a hot day, either cancel the hike or make sure you choose to Nordic hike during the coolest time of the day. Think about choosing a route that offers some shade from trees.

Advantages of a Map and Compass

The one- to three-hour-long trails recommended for Nordic walking or hiking are well marked. If you are not an expert in reading an orienteering compass or using a topographical map, stay on those marked trails even though you may get tempted to go off a trail. Usually marked trails are maintained well. But never rely only on the signs. If the trail has not been maintained properly, signs may have been turned around. Bring current information such as maps from trail guidebooks or directly from the staff at local outdoor adventure stores. Some destinations even offer a private tour guide, which is always the best thing to do when visiting a new place. Private tours ensure that you see all the best things in the area. Just make sure it is a legitimate business.

In addition to offering books on trails, the local outdoor retailers may offer other useful outdoor training. It is always a good idea to know as much as you can about outdoor life before heading out on a trail. Taking classes in reading maps and using a compass and GPS are all helpful tools in knowing your location to prevent getting lost. GPS should be used as a supplement to maps and compasses.

If you don't know how to use an orienteering compass, just purchase a simple one, which indicates only the four distinct directions: north, south, east, and west. Before you start the route, establish north, south, east, and west. Determine where you are located at the start based on the map on the board. The board should have the four directions. Hold the compass level and make it a part of you. When you turn, the direction will change with you. Now line up with the map and check the direction of your starting location compared to the route. If you head out and you get uneasy about walking back in the correct direction, just take a look at the compass. If your starting location was

SAFETY TIP
When Nordic walking or hiking, stay on wide and well-marked trails.

south of the route and you are walking south, you are walking back in the correct direction. Of course, it gets tricky if the route changes directions. Most trails are shaped as a loop, so note every turn and write down the direction from there to your starting location. If you learn to use maps and orienteering compasses together, you can navigate routes more professionally. Until then, stay on marked and well-maintained trails.

Seven Nordic Walking Wonders Worldwide

Nordic walkers worldwide were asked to contribute their favorite walks in and around their cities to help you get started in creating your own Nordic walking routes. The estimated time for the distance of each route is based on an average speed. All the local trails are focused on marked and wide trails (no off trails) from one to three hours in length. The difficulty levels are expected to be easy, moderate, or difficult; but after reading chapters 7, 8, and 9, you will know how to vary the intensity yourself. If you get hit by the travel bug while reading about the various cities and countries, appendix B has more resources for Nordic walking activities around the world.

Nordic Walking Wonder 1

Country: USA

City and state: Santa Monica, California

City Web site: www.smgov.net

About the city: Santa Monica is a walking- and biking-friendly community in Southern California, mainly known for its skateboarding and surfing culture. With a population of close to 90,000, it is located in a beautiful bay with a wide sandy beach overlooking the coastal Santa Monica Mountains. There are approximately 325 sunny days. Morning fog is common from May through July. It is a peaceful but progressive community surrounded by the city of Los Angeles to the north, east, and south. Because the city is so close to Hollywood, film productions are a common sight. The entrance to the Santa Monica Pier is a famous landmark on and off screen. Just south of the pier is the birthplace of the 20th-century fitness boom. No wonder that this is the place where Nordic walking was introduced in North America!

SAFETY TIP

Find out ahead of time the distance of a walk, the time it will take to walk it, whether there is any elevation, and what type of terrain to expect.

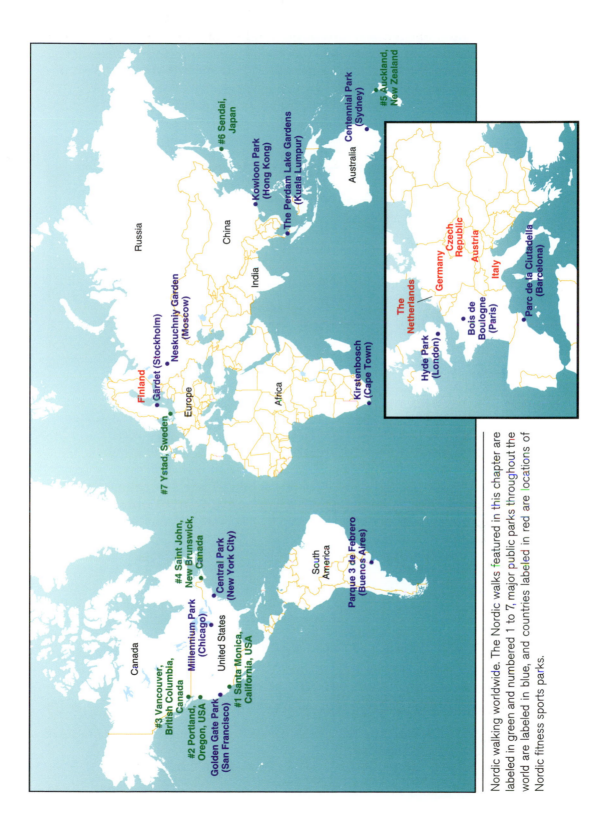

Nordic walking worldwide. The Nordic walks featured in this chapter are labeled in green and numbered 1 to 7; major public parks throughout the world are labeled in blue, and countries labeled in red are locations of Nordic fitness sports parks.

Map labels (green, numbered Nordic walks):
- #1 Santa Monica, California, USA
- #2 Portland, Oregon, USA
- #3 Vancouver, British Columbia, Canada
- #4 Saint John, New Brunswick, Canada
- #5 Auckland, New Zealand
- #6 Sendai, Japan
- #7 Ystad, Sweden

Map labels (blue, major public parks):
- Golden Gate Park (San Francisco)
- Millennium Park (Chicago)
- Central Park (New York City)
- Parque 3 de Febrero (Buenos Aires)
- Gärdet (Stockholm)
- Neskuchniy Garden (Moscow)
- Kirstenbosch (Cape Town)
- Kowloon Park (Hong Kong)
- The Perdam Lake Gardens (Kuala Lumpur)
- Centennial Park (Sydney)
- Hyde Park (London)
- Bois de Boulogne (Paris)
- Parc de la Ciutadella (Barcelona)

Map labels (red, countries with Nordic fitness sports parks):
- Finland
- The Netherlands
- Germany
- Czech Republic
- Austria
- Italy

Map labels (black, geographic):
Russia, China, India, Europe, Africa, Australia, Canada, United States, South America

Map: Print a map from the Web site www.smgov.net or pick up a map at the Santa Monica visitor information kiosk located just north of the pier on 1400 Ocean Avenue, Santa Monica, CA 90401 (phone 310-393-7593). It's open daily 10 a.m. to 4 p.m.

A Nordic Walk in the City

Location: Santa Monica Beach

Start to finish: Start at the pier, which is located at the end of Colorado Avenue and Ocean Avenue. Head down the hill toward the pier. At the bottom of the hill, make a left and pass the famous carousel. Go down the wooden stairs and make a right. You are now walking south. After you pass some gorgeous beach hotels (Hotel Casa del Mar is the last one), you will stay to the right and

Santa Monica Beach.

cross the biking path. Be careful when crossing. In-line skaters and bikers enjoy the no-traffic path, so their speeds tend to be quite high. Enter the path closest to the beach. This is designated for walkers. Continue heading south. So far it has all been asphalt or cement. If you want to try sand, just step right out into the sand. Walk for another 15 to 20 minutes until you come to the last parking lot on your left. Now you have three options:

1. You can turn around and walk the same route back to the pier.

2. You can cross the biking path and walk east toward Main Street, which is one of the three main shopping areas in Santa Monica. After you cross the bike path, continue on a path and pass the playground on your right. Cross Barnard Way and continue east on a path that runs through a small green park called Ocean View Park. This path turns into a street called Ashland. Continue on Ashland until you come to Main Street. Make a left and walk back to Colorado Avenue. Make a left on Colorado Avenue and you will be back at the pier.

3. Or continue south to Venice, which is people-watching paradise with funky stores.

Estimated distance and time: 2.2 miles (3.5 km), 30 to 45 minutes (option 1)

Difficulty level: Easy on the asphalt, difficult on the soft sand

Terrain: Flat

Surface: Asphalt but access to grass and sand

Other information and tips: If you are driving, you can find metered street parking around the pier or continue down Colorado onto the pier to park on the pier deck or nearby beach parking for a fee. Any gray color on the map on the Web site that says "lot" means it is a parking lot with a fee. There are plenty of public restrooms along the boardwalk. If you want to explore some hills, you can continue on Ashland (option 2) after crossing Main Street. That whole area is called Ocean Park. Besides being a historic district, it offers some great hills, from Main Street (west) to Lincoln Boulevard (east) and Pico (north) to Rose Avenue (south). Refer to the map on the Web site at www.smgov.net.

A Nordic Walk in a Grassy City Park

Location: Palisades Park

Start to finish: Start at the pier, which is located at the end of Colorado Avenue and Ocean Avenue. Stay on Ocean Avenue and walk north in the park called Palisades Park. It is a somewhat narrow park with an incredible view of the Pacific Ocean and the Santa Monica Mountains. After 0.7 mile (1.1 km) when you cross California Avenue, it gets wider. At the very end of the park is a totem pole. Turn around and

Palisades Park in Santa Monica.

return to the starting point at the pier.

Estimated distance and time: 3 miles (4.8 km), 45 to 60 minutes

Difficulty level: Easy

Terrain: Flat

Surface: Grass but access to a walking path that changes from asphalt to dirt

Other information and tips: Palisades Park is located in downtown Santa Monica and it runs parallel for four blocks to the famous 3rd Street Promenade, which is closed off from traffic.

If you want to add some more hills, continue on the street after the park ends. This is Ocean Avenue. It takes you down to Santa Monica Canyon. At the bottom, turn around and head back up. This adds another 0.6 mile (1 km) to your walk.

If you would like to add yet another hill, head west on California Avenue. It takes you down to PCH (Pacific Coast Highway). At the bottom of the hill, turn around and head back up the same way. This adds another 0.6 mile (1 km) to your walk.

A Nordic Hike in the Local Mountains

Location: Temescal Gateway Park

Start to finish: After you park the car, walk toward the end of the parking lot. See the following driving directions. To get to the trailhead, continue past the Temescal Camp Store and stay to the left another 50 yards (46 m). Step off the asphalt path and onto the dirt and head up the wooden stairs. In a few minutes you will see a sign to the right. Choose the Temescal

Temescal Gateway Park in Pacific Palisades.

Canyon Trail, which is 2.6 miles (4.2 km). This trail is a loop, and if you start to the left (the Temescal Ridge trail), it takes you rapidly up a steep and long hill, which you will come back down on. Start to the right and head toward the waterfall, which is about 1 mile (1.6 km). A few minutes into the hike, you will cross a service road. Veer to the right and then make an immediate left. Stay on this path to the waterfall, which is a moderate climb. Take a moment to enjoy the waterfall from the little bridge. After a nice break, head up the same path for about 10 minutes until you reach a sign saying "To Sunset Blvd." Make a left and stay on this main path for the rest of the hike. If you become hesitant, always stay to the left. After a few minutes you will have reached the top. It is time for another break to enjoy a view of the Pacific Ocean. Check the time it took you to the top. You have about the same amount of time left, but now it is all downhill. As you descend, it will get technical in some places with pebbles and small rocks. Watch your step. In some places you will have an incredible view of the city of Los Angeles and smaller surrounding cities like Santa Monica. As you come closer to the start of the trailhead, you will pass the same sign where you chose the Temescal Canyon Trail. Stay to the left and continue down the same wooden stairs to reach the starting and finishing place.

Estimated distance and time: 2.6 miles (4.2 km), 1 to 1.5 hours

Elevation: Highest point 200 feet (61 m)

Difficulty level: Moderate to difficult

Terrain: Hilly

Surface: Dirt with some small rocks and pebbles

Driving directions from the city: From the Santa Monica Pier, continue north on Ocean Avenue. Stay in the left lane. Make a left on California Avenue. At the bottom of the hill, make a right onto PCH (Pacific Coast Highway) heading toward Malibu. After a little less than 2 miles (3.2 km), make a right on Temescal Canyon and head up a long hill for about 1 mile (1.6 km). Cross Sunset Boulevard and enter the park. The self-parking fee was $5 in 2008. It's about a 10-minute drive from the pier.

Other information and tips: Stay on the main path to avoid poison oak, ticks, and rattlesnakes.

At the end of the parking lot of the Temescal Gateway Park is a store with maps, water, and snacks (Temescal Camp Store). Next to it you will find restrooms. This is a popular park within the Santa Monica Mountains because it is so close to the city, yet if offers the perfect getaway feeling from the big city. Thanks to oak and sycamore trees, it has some shady parts. For more information, visit www.lamountains.com/parks.asp?parkid=58. Make sure you pay the self-parking fee to avoid getting a ticket. Just put $5 in the envelope by the sign "Pay Here" and enter the date and your license number of the car. Tear one part off to put on the dashboard inside the car. Drop the envelope in the designated slot.

No car? No problem! Rent a bike at any Perry's Café located along the beach (see www.perryscafe.com/find.html). No bikes are allowed on the highway, but you can use the beach biking path that runs parallel to the PCH. Access the biking path from the Santa Monica Pier on the beach side and head north toward Malibu.

The Nordic walks were created by Malin Svensson, Santa Monica, California, USA.

Nordic Walking Wonder 2

Country: USA

City and state: Portland, Oregon

City Web site: www.travelportland.com

About the city: Portland is located about 43 miles (70 km) inland from the west coast of the United States. Canada borders to the north. It is a beautiful city with great public transit and a population of about 570,000. Portland is known as the City of Roses and is the home of the NBA Trail Blazers team. It is also known for its many microbreweries.

Map: Pick up a map at Portland Visitors Association (701 SW 6th Ave #1, Portland, OR 97204, 503-275-8358) and get ready to go Nordic walking in Portland.

A Nordic Walk in the City

Location: Waterfront Bridge Loop

Start to finish: Start at the River Place Marina at 315 SW Montgomery Street. Plenty of parking garages are available, and the area is serviced by the Portland Streetcar. Head north on Tom McCall Waterfront Park and continue down to the Steel Bridge. Cross over the Willamette River using the Steel Bridge. You will now be on the East Side Esplanade, a great trail that runs beside and sometimes on the river. Head south on the esplanade

Waterfront Bridge Loop in Portland.

until you reach the Hawthorne Bridge. Cross back over the river and turn left (south) and return to the marina. Plenty of restaurants and cafés are there to refresh you after your walk.

Estimated distance and time: 3.7 miles (6 km), 1 hour

Difficulty level: Easy

Terrain: Flat

Surface: Asphalt

Other information and tips: For a more challenging city walk, less than a mile away from the marina is Duniway Park at SW 6th Avenue and Sheridan Street. Start at Duniway Park and head up Terwilliger Boulevard all the way to Barbur Boulevard; turn around and head back to Duniway Park. If you are too tired for the hill, you can turn left on Barbur Boulevard and return to Duniway Park using Barbur Boulevard. But if you are ready for the hill again, it is a much more scenic walk heading back using Terwilliger. It's a good climb up Terwilliger, and you will be rewarded by exceptional views of the city and the surrounding mountains. This is a very popular trail that is well maintained and has restrooms and water stops.

Estimated distance and time: 6.5 miles (10.5 km), 2 hours

Difficulty level: Moderate

Terrain: Hilly

Surface: Asphalt

For more information on Duniway Park, visit the Web site at www.portlandonline.com/parks/finder/index.cfm?PropertyID=44&action=ViewPark.

A Nordic Walk in a Grassy City Park

Location: Tom McCall Waterfront Park

Start to finish: Start at the River Place Marina at 315 SW Montgomery Street. Plenty of parking garages are available, and the area is serviced by the Portland Streetcar. Head north on Tom McCall Waterfront Park using the grass fields. Continue to the turnaround at the Steel Bridge and return to the marina.

Tom McCall Waterfront Park in Portland.

Estimated distance and time: 3.5 miles (5.6 km), 1 hour

Difficulty level: Easy

Terrain: Flat

Surface: Grass and asphalt

Other information and tips: A walk on the weekend from April to October will allow you to visit Saturday Market, an outdoor arts and food fair featuring local products. Saturday Market is located across from the north end of Tom McCall Waterfront Park. Definitely give it a try. Saturday Market is a real taste of Portland. Various outdoor concerts and fairs are hosted in the park, making it a hub of activity during the summer months.

Tom McCall Park stretches through several sections of Portland. Venturing into the city from the park will give you access to a host of restaurants, shopping, and activities in several sections of the city, including the shopping district, Old Town, and China Town. For more information on Tom McCall Waterfront Park, visit the Web site at www.portlandonline.com/parks/finder/index.cfm?PropertyID=156&action=ViewPark.

A Nordic Hike in the Local Mountains

Location: Forest Park

Start to finish: Drive or take the bus to the end of NW Thurman Road. This is the beginning of the Leif Erikson Trail. See the following driving directions. This trail is very wide and has mile markers every half mile. You can pick a mile marker to turn around at and tailor your walk to the distance you would like to go. For a more challenging

Forest Park in Portland.

hike, you can branch off onto the Wildwood Trail that crosses Leif Erikson in several spots. Wildwood is a much hillier and narrower trail, but there are several places where Nordic walkers can walk side by side. The entire length of Leif Erikson allows side-by-side walking. If you feel lost or too challenged while on Wildwood, you can take any of the fire service roads back to Leif Erikson Trail and head back. You will cross numbered fire service roads every mile or so.

Estimated distance and time: 11.2 miles (18 km) one way and 22.4 miles (36 km) round-trip, 5 to 6 hours round-trip

Elevation: 100 feet (30 m), mostly a forested sea-level hike with elevation gain of 700 feet and a loss of only a few hundred feet several times during the walk

Difficulty levels: Easy to moderate (Leif Erikson), moderate to advanced (Wildwood)

Terrain: Hilly forested trail

Surface: Dirt

Driving directions from the city: Forest Park is in the city of Portland. Just take your car or a bus to the end of NW Thurman Road. This is the trailhead for the Leif Erikson Trail.

Other information and tips: Portland has the largest natural forested area within city limits in the United States. It has more than 5,100 wooded acres with over 75 miles of marked and maintained trails. Once you have experienced Forest Park, you will want to explore all the trails. Maps and information are available at the Friends of Forest Park at www.friendsofforestpark.org.

The Nordic walks were created by Gary Johnson, Portland, Oregon, USA.

Nordic Walking Wonder 3

Country: Canada

City and province: Vancouver, British Columbia

City Web site: www.vancouver.com

About the city: Vancouver is about 310 miles (500 km) north of Portland and has an estimated population of 600,000. It is the largest city in British Columbia, a province that is not only the third largest in Canada but also home to almost a fourth of the ancient temperate rain forests left in the world. This natural beauty is surrounded by water on three sides and has a mild climate year-round. Vancouverites have a healthy, outdoor-oriented lifestyle. Vancouver will be hosting the 2010 Winter Olympic Games.

Map: Pick up a map at the tourist information office at Tourism Vancouver at Waterfront Centre (200 Burrard Street, phone 604-683-2000) and get ready to go Nordic walking in Vancouver.

A Nordic Walk in the City

Location: English Bay Walk

Start to finish: Start outside the entrance to Stanley Park's Outdoor Swimming Pool situated at Second Beach, where the seawall (walking path) can be joined. Continue south on the seawall trail with the sea to your right (west) and the children's park to your left (east). Stay on the designated side for walkers and runners. The other side of the path is for cyclists. Continue past the Sylvia Hotel on your left where you will see plenty of restaurants and cafés. Here English Bay Beach is a great place for people watching, looking at boats, or spotting the odd harbor seal emerging to the surface for air. Continue along the seawall toward Burrard Bridge. The road of traffic rises above you to the left on Beach Avenue. It leaves a sloping bank of grass, where more people can pass the time away. Continue until you reach the small ferry stop where you can catch a ferry to Granville Island for some shopping or lunch. Now turn around and retrace your steps and feel the invigorating wind on your face and adding intensity to your walk.

English Bay Walk in Vancouver.

Estimated distance and time: approximately 3 miles (4.8 km), 1 hour

Difficulty level: Easy (seawall), moderate (beach)

Terrain: Flat

Surface: Asphalt (seawall) and sand (beach if the tide is out)

Other information and tips: The seawall (a wall made to break the force of the waves and to protect the shore from erosion) surrounds Stanley Park and shapes this peninsula located in the northern corner of central Vancouver. The seawall continues just southwest of Stanley Park, around English Bay, and farther south to False Creek; it ends at the University of British Columbia, located on the northwest tip of Vancouver. This part of the seawall provides the people of Vancouver with approximately 15 miles (25 km) of asphalt path to walk on.

Hourly and daily parking rates are in effect year-round. You can find pay parking by driving around Stanley Park's one-way road called Park Drive until you reach the signs for Second Beach, where there is ample parking in a bay at the side of the road and more behind these spaces in a small parking lot. Avoid crowds by arriving before 11 a.m. and leaving late. There are plenty of restrooms and places to eat.

If the tide is out, you can access the beach at the beginning of the walk at Second Beach and continue along English Bay Beach and Sunset Beach. Step up onto the seawall whenever the trail in front of you gets too congested with stones or the logs that casually float in with the tide in Vancouver. Walking on the sand will increase the intensity of your walk.

A Nordic Walk in a City Park

Location: Stanley Park

Start to finish: Start the walk at Third Beach, which is located on the west side of the park just above Ferguson Point. Head east to cross the main road, Park Drive, to join Rawlings Trail; walk south until you come to Lovers Walk, where you make a left (east). This trail will eventually join Squirrel Trail, which leads you over a footbridge above Stanley Park Causeway, a main road into and out of Vancouver. Continue downward to Beaver Lake to walk around the lake. Enjoy the pond flowers and wildlife that inhabit it. Turn around to return to your starting point.

Estimated distance and time: 3.1 miles (5 km), 1 hour

Difficulty level: Easy

Terrain: Winding forest trail

Surface: Dirt and gravel

Stanley Park in Vancouver.

Other information and tips: If you need a map, go north on Georgia Street and enter Stanley Park. There is a granite-fronted information booth where you can pick up a free map of the park.

Surrounded by Douglas fir, Western hemlock, and Western red cedar, this park is full of wildlife such as raccoons, squirrels, and coyotes. Stanley Park invites people to Nordic walk on its endless paths. Winter can be wet in Vancouver, although the scenery is worth it. Waterproof gear is a must. Summer can be hot, and walking under the trees brings a relief in the midday sun.

Some trails allow bikes. There are many trails in Stanley Park if you wish to lengthen or shorten your walk. Should you tire on the way and want to return quickly, a free tourist bus circulates around Stanley Island that will take you back to your starting point.

For more information, visit www.city.vancouver.bc.ca/Parks/parks/stanley or www.city.vancouver.bc.ca/Parks/parks/stanley/gettingthere.htm.

A Nordic Hike in the Local Mountains

Location: Baden-Powell Trail

Start to finish: It can be accessed from several points. Beginning from the trail's most westerly point at Eagleridge, walkers ascend about 3,740 feet (1,140 m) to the top of Black Mountain in Cypress Provincial Park. From there, the Baden-Powell trail descends toward the charming village of Deep Cove. Savor breathtaking views of Vancouver as you traverse through densely forested trails past trickling streams and rocky bluffs. The trail is well marked with bright orange triangular tags on trees.

Estimated distance and time: 25 miles total (40 km), about 10 hours for the entire trail (see notes in "Other information and tips" section)

Elevation: Elevation gain close to Deep Cove is 500 feet (152 m); total elevation gain on the trail is 3,740 feet (1,140 m)

Difficulty: Moderate

Terrain: Hilly mountain path

Surface: Dirt (snow at higher elevations in the winter)

Driving directions from the city: From Vancouver, head over the Lions Gate Bridge, located at the north end of Stanley Park, and drive toward the Municipality of West Vancouver. At the intersection of Taylor Way and Marine Drive, go right on Taylor Way up to the Highway 1 access. Drive west on Highway 1 and exit at the Eagleridge exit. At the top of the exit ramp, turn right into a cul-de-sac and start walking. There is ample free parking in this cul-de-sac.

Other information and tips: Baden-Powell Trail is a major hiking and walking route in the North Shore Mountain trail system. It extends all the way from Horseshoe Bay (west) to Deep Cove (east). Since it is not intended as one long hike but rather as several shorter ones, it can be accessed from several points. There are a variety of entry points, such as Eagleridge, Lynn Canyon Park, Seymour Provincial Park, and Skyline Road. For more information, call the District of North Vancouver Parks at 604-990-3800 and follow the prompts to the Baden-Powell Trail. Also visit the Web site http://vancouver-canada.ca/baden/badenpowell.htm.

The Baden-Powell Trail is named after Lord Baden-Powell, founder of the world Scout Movement.

The Nordic walks were created by Paula Artley and Alastair and Suzanne Campbell, Vancouver, British Columbia, Canada.

Nordic Walking Wonder 4

Country: Canada

City and province: Saint John, New Brunswick

City Web site: www.saintjohn.ca

About the city: About 600 miles (965 km) northeast of New York City (northeast coast of the United States), is a picturesque coastal Canadian city called Saint John, with an estimated population of 60,000. The province of New Brunswick borders the northern part of Maine, a northeastern state in the United States. Saint John is located right next to the Bay of Fundy ("deep river"), which has the highest tides in the world and is only an hour's drive from the Maine border. Saint John is known for its pristine parks, steep history-lined streets, and fine dining and shopping. It offers a vibrant art and entertainment community with colorful festivals and an unforgettable ocean adventure with attractions around every turn.

Map: Pick up a map at the Barber's General Store (open seasonally) at Market Slip at the bottom of King Street at the corner of Water Street, and get ready to go Nordic walking in Saint John.

A Nordic Walk in the City

Location: Harbour Passage

Start to finish: Leave from Market Square (a shopping mall) at the base of King Street and St. Patrick Street. Proceed outside along the harbor on the wooden boardwalk of the Hilton Hotel to Harbour Passage. Harbour Passage is a paved walkway (cranberry in color) with historic sites. Pass under the big bridge to the foot of Bentley Street, where there's a beautiful lookout through

Reversing Falls Bridge in Saint John.

the narrows into the Bay of Fundy. Walk a little farther to the end of the cranberry trail along the sidewalk on Chesley Drive, up the hill, and across the Reversing Falls Bridge to the Reversing Falls restaurant and lookout (total 2.1 miles, or 3.5 km). After a rest, turn back, but this time turn left on Douglas Avenue and walk along a sidewalk past beautiful Victorian and Edwardian homes. At the end of this street, turn right on Main Street along the right-side sidewalk, over the viaduct (which crosses over the highway), and back to Market Square where you started.

Estimated distance and time: 4.2 miles (7 km), 1.5 hours as a leisurely walk

Difficulty level: Easy to moderate

Terrain: Mostly flat with one large hill

Surface: Asphalt

Other information and tips: You will share the cranberry trail with cyclists. One side is designated for walkers and the other is for cyclists, so don't forget to leave room. You may take this walk on a day when cruise ships are visiting the city, so there's *a lot* to look at along this harbor walk: people, fishing boats, seals, and beautiful scenery.

A Nordic Walk on a Sandy Beach

Location: New River Beach

Start to finish: Once you arrive at this provincial park (see driving directions), park in one of the parking lots. New River Beach is a breathtaking spot on the Bay of Fundy coast. It is a wonderful beach walk by the bay with beautiful large homes on the tops of the hillsides. Walk as far as you can on the beach and then turn around to the starting point.

New River Beach in Saint John.

Estimated distance and time: Approximately 2.8 miles (4.5 km), 45 minutes

Difficulty level: Easy

Terrain: Flat

Surface: Compact sand (compact because of tides)

Driving directions: New River Beach is about a 20-minute drive from downtown Saint John. Start at Market Square and head west on Route 1 and follow the signs to New River Beach, which is a provincial park.

Other information and tips: This beach is in a provincial park, which means it is owned and run by the government. You will be sharing it only with picnickers and campers. There aren't many swimmers because the temperature varies only about 4 degrees Celsius from winter to summer. The water is very cold all year. It's only for Nordic Vikings!

A Nordic Hike in the Local Mountains

Location: Fundy Trail

Start to finish: An hour outside Saint John, you will find this hilly trail that wraps around the coast of the Bay of Fundy. (See driving directions.) Start the walk from the parking lot, just past the entrance to the park, and follow the Fundy Trail sign. The trail is wide and beautifully groomed with breathtaking views of waterfalls, the ocean, and lots of wildlife. There are steep hills as well as flat areas. Restrooms and water are available along the route. At the end is a pavilion where food is sold and a shuttle bus can take you back if desired. If you turn around and walk back to the starting point, you will have covered approximately 13 miles (22 km).

Estimated distance and time: 6.5 miles (11 km) one way to the pavilion (13 miles or 22 km round-trip), about 3 hours one way (an option is to take the shuttle bus back to your car)

Elevation: Sea level to over 500 feet (152 m)

Difficulty level: Moderate to difficult

Terrain: Hilly

Surface: Dirt and gravel

Driving directions from the city: From Saint John, drive east about 40 minutes along Loch Lomond Road, past the airport to St. Martins (Route 111). Once in St. Martins, continue along the same road through two very picturesque covered bridges for another 20 minutes to the Fundy Trail. Parking lots are available at the gates of the parkway. Visit http://fundytrailparkway.com/directions.htm for more information.

Other information and tips: For an additional adventure, you can continue on a more challenging trail from the pavilion up the mountain to another bungalow; the first one is the interpretation centre at the end of the trail with or without a guide. To get there, you must cross a rope bridge. For more information about this adventure, visit the interpretation centre in the pavilion.

The hilliest areas of the hike are paved to reduce landslides. They are very, very steep, so using poles makes it easier.

Bring food and water with you so that you can really enjoy the views. This is a place where you want to give yourself lots of time to take it all in. It's truly spectacular, even to those who live there.

In St. Martins you'll find the best fish and chips close to the covered bridges in one of the two diners located along the beach there, so remember that after your hike. There are also caves to discover on the same beach as the diners. Leave yourself some energy to explore them.

The Nordic walks were created by Marilyn Inch, Saint John, New Brunswick, Canada.

Nordic Walking Wonder 5

Country: New Zealand

Region: North Island

City: Auckland

City Web sites: www.aucklandcity.govt.nz

www.arc.govt.nz

About the city: Auckland is the largest city in New Zealand, located on the North Island with a population of 1.2 million. The landscape of the city is formed by 49 extinct volcanoes, which are now largely grassed hills and water-filled basins. It is called the "City of Sails" because the harbor has more boats per capita than any other city in the world. Cricket and rugby are the most popular sports. The Maori people are the natives of New Zealand, and you can feel their rich culture everywhere you go.

Map: Pick up a map in the atrium of the Sky Tower, located on the corner of Victoria and Federal Streets, and get ready to go Nordic walking in Auckland. (You can also pick up a map at the Auckland International Airport terminal.)

A Nordic Walk in the City

Location: Albert Park to the Auckland Domain

Start to finish: Start in Albert Park. It is located on top of Victoria Street, which is a major intersecting road off the main street of Queen Street. Walk in a circuit around the park and exit onto Princes Street and the Auckland University campus. Head northeast and walk down Alfred Street. Continue down Grafton Road past the School of Business to the Auckland Domain, which is the largest park within

Albert Park in Auckland.

the city. Enter at Lower Domain Drive and walk uphill on the Centennial Hill path. Look to your left for the wonderful sculptures placed on the grass. At the top of the hill you have the option of commencing a park circuit or continuing ahead to the museum. Return to Albert Park using the same route.

Estimated distance and time: 3.7 miles (6 km), 1 hour (round-trip)

Difficulty level: Easy to moderate

Terrain: Flat with one good hill

Surface: Asphalt and grass with a mixture of paths and roadways

Other information and tips: Albert Park and the Auckland Domain are two parks situated within New Zealand's largest city of Auckland, providing an inner-city sanctuary for nature lovers. Easily accessible from within the central business district, this round-trip walk showcases formal gardens, ponds, the Wintergardens, sculptures, green spaces, and historical buildings without the worry of traffic, dogs, or cyclists. The Auckland Museum provides visitors with an insight into New Zealand Maori (indigenous) culture and an extensive Polynesian collection. Both parks and the museum are accessible year-round.

A Nordic Walk in a Grassy City Park

Location: Cornwall Park including One Tree Hill summit

Start to finish: Start your walk at the gates along the avenue lined with native Pohutukawa trees (Pohutukawa Drive). Continue to walk straight ahead at the roundabout and take the doubletree-lined pathway (grass or asphalt) of Twin Oaks Drive. At the end of this drive, look to your right for the magnificent volcanic cone topped with an obelisk. This is the One Tree Hill summit. A grass track will lead you up the side of the cone at this point. You may also continue to follow the roadway, which gently rises toward the summit. The final section (920 feet, or 280 meters) is a steep climb up to the obelisk. Magnificent citywide views make this climb worth the effort. Watch for cars on the final leg to the summit. Return using the same route.

Cornwall Park including One Tree Hill summit in Auckland.

Estimated distance and time: 5 miles (8 km), 1.5 hours (round-trip)

Difficulty level: Easy to moderate

Terrain: Flat and hilly

Surface: Asphalt pathways, roadways, and grass

Driving directions: Take the Southern Motorway from Auckland City and travel south to the Greenlane exit. Follow the roundabout to the right and exit onto Greenlane Road East. Pass through two sets of traffic lights. The main entrance to Cornwall Park is at the third set. Turn left through the stone gates marked Cornwall Park. Parking is available immediately inside the gates or in a large car park area at the end of the avenue.

Other information and tips: The climb up to the 280-meter One Tree Hill summit requires a good fitness level for a 10- to 15-minute climb on a good road or up a grass pathway.

An extensive park and farmlands, 10 minutes from central Auckland, One Tree Hill (Maori name, Maungakiekie) is a prominent landmark and one of the largest of Auckland's 49 volcanic cones. Sadly, the lone tree that was featured side by side with the obelisk was removed some years ago for safety and cultural reasons. It is hoped that it will be replaced. Walk among groves of native and exotic trees, grazing cattle, and sheep. You can walk extensively along grass pathways without paws or with paws along the many asphalt paths and roads, which intertwine throughout the park. It is accessible year-round. Visit www.cornwallpark.co.nz for more information.

A Nordic Hike in the Local Mountains

Location: Cascades and Montana Heritage Walk

Start to finish: The best place to start a walk is at the Arataki Information Centre on Scenic Drive, Waitakere, where maps and historical information on the main tracks and walks are available. The Cascades walk is 4.3 miles (7 km) from the information centre. The start of the walk is in a park off Te Henga Road in the Waitakere Ranges and shares its entrance with a golf course. The park has several walks that include circular routes and out-and-back courses. One of the most popular walks is the Cascades and Montana Heritage Walk, an out-and-back walk. All tracks are signposted and marked.

Estimated distance and time: 6.2 miles (10 km), approximately 2 to 3 hours

Montana Heritage Walk in Cascade Kauri.

Elevation: Not assessed

Difficulty level: Moderate to difficult

Terrain: Easy to challenging grades

Surface: Soil, grass, and some boardwalk

Driving directions from the city: The Montana Heritage Trail is located at Cascade Kauri, which is a 15-mile (25 km) or 40-minute drive from downtown Auckland. Follow the northwestern motorway (State Highway 16) to the Lincoln Road exit. Turn left onto Lincoln Road and take a right turn onto Universal Drive. At the roundabout, take the third exit onto Swanson Road and continue straight ahead onto Scenic Drive. Continue along Scenic Drive to the information centre or turn right into Te Henga Road and then left onto Falls Road to go directly to the Montana Walk. Drive through the Waitakere Golf Course, past the clubhouse, to the car park at the end of the road.

Other information and tips: It is recommended that you visit the Arataki Information Centre on Scenic Drive, Waitakere, where maps and historical information on the main tracks and walks are available. This is 4.3 miles (7 km) from the Cascades Walk.

The boardwalk is suitable for poles with and without asphalt paws.

The Waitakere Ranges extend over 18.6 miles (30 km) along the west coast of Auckland. At the northern end is the Montana Heritage and Cascade Kauri and Fairy Falls walk. The majestic kauri trees were milled extensively through the ranges in the late 1800s and, fortunately, the regrowth is now well established. There is a mixture of new forest along with areas of the ancient forest and some of the old giant kauri trees spared by the foresters. The walks also lead to freshwater streams and beautiful waterfalls. The park itself has several picnic areas. Visit www.arc.govt.nz/parks/our-parks/parks-in-the-region/cascades for more information.

The Nordic walks were created by June Stevenson, Auckland, New Zealand.

Nordic Walking Wonder 6

Country: Japan

Prefecture: Miyagi

City: Sendai

City Web sites: www.city.sendai.jp/index-e.html

www.sentabi.jp/1000/10000000.html

www.stcb.or.jp/eng/index.html

About the city: Sendai city is located 15 miles (25 km) from the northeast coast of Japan and 217 miles (350 km) north of Tokyo. Take the express train (Shinkansen) from Tokyo, and you will be in Sendai in 100 minutes. The population is about 1 million. Sendai is well known as the "City of Trees" because of its tree-lined avenues. In mid-April you will experience the well-known and beautiful cherry blossoms, sakura, which can be interpreted as new beginnings.

Map: Pick up a map of the city at the Maruzen bookstore in the AER Building (address is AER Building 1F, 1-3-1, Chuo, Aoba-ku, Sendai). It is only a two-minute walk from the JR (Japan Railway) Sendai station. Now you are ready to go Nordic walking in Sendai.

A Nordic Walk in the City

Location: Shiroishi River

Start to finish: Go to the Sendai station, the main railway station of the city. Take the Tohoku-honsen Line train and get off at the Funaoka station. Exit the station via the pedestrian overpass called Sakura Hodokyo. Nordic walk by the Shiroishi River to the Ohgawara station. Return on the same route.

Estimated distance and time: 1.8 miles (3 km), 40 minutes

Difficulty level: Easy

Terrain: Flat

Surface: Asphalt

Shiroishi River walkway in Sendai.

Other information and tips: The most wonderful time to go Nordic walking by the Shiroishi River is in mid-April when the cherry trees blossom. Imagine walking under a cherry blossom umbrella for more than a mile (2 km).

A Nordic Walk in a Grassy City Park

Location: Dainohara Forest Park

Start to finish: Follow the signs at the Sendai station to the subway. Take the subway toward Izumi-chuo. Get off at the Asahigaoka station. The Dainohara Forest Park is next to the station. You can start Nordic walking counterclockwise or clockwise around the park.

Estimated distance and time: 1.9 miles (3 km) one loop, 40 minutes

Dainohara Forest Park in Sendai.

Difficulty level: Moderate

Terrain: Flat and hilly

Surface: Dirt, asphalt (path), and grass

Other information and tips: The whole park becomes ablaze with autumn leaves at the end of October. You can see beautiful red and yellow leaves.

A Nordic Hike in the Local Mountains

Location: Greenpia Iwanuma

Start to finish: You can get a Nordic walking map at the office of Greenpia Iwanuma and enjoy Nordic walking and hiking on several trails. There are spots from where you can see Japanese rice fields, mountain landscapes, and the Pacific Ocean.

Estimated distance and time: Maximum 4.3 miles (7 km), 1.5 hours

Elevation: 492 feet (150 m)

Difficulty level: Easy to moderate

Terrain: Hilly

Surface: Grass, dirt, and asphalt

Directions from the city: Go to the Sendai station, the main railway station of the city. Take the Tohoku-honsen Line train and get off at the Iwanuma station (20 minutes). Go to the bus stop on the east side of the station. Take the bus to Greenpia Iwanuma (20 minutes) either via the South-North line or the West line.

Greenpia Iwanuma.

Other information and tips: There are some facilities you can use before or after Nordic walking, such as a swimming pool, hot springs, and restaurant.

The Nordic walks were created by Naohiro Takahashi, Sendai, Miyagi, Japan.

Nordic Walking Wonder 7

Country: Sweden

City: Ystad

City Web site: www.ystad.se

About the city: Ystad is the southernmost city in Sweden located next to the Baltic Sea (Östersjön). Compared to other places along the same latitude, it offers a mild climate year-round. In 40 minutes by train you can enjoy Malmö, the third-largest city of Sweden. In just one hour you can be in Copenhagen, Denmark, and the international airport, Kastrup. A ferry from Ystad will take you straight to Poland or to a picturesque Danish island. The permanent population is around 18,000, but this number doubles easily in the summertime. It is the perfect summer retreat with beaches, forests, and sport activities, including golf. You can walk or bike to everything. It is a fairy-tale medieval town with cobblestones, half-timbered houses, and buildings dating from the 13th century. The most popular sport is handboll, and the team Ystad IF plays in the highest-ranked series in Sweden. Ystad is internationally known from the series of detective novels by Henning Mankell. The main character in the books, Kurt Wallander, is the inspector of the police in Ystad.

Map: Pick up a map at Ystad Turistbyrå (tourist center) located in the art museum, a red brick building at the north side of St Knuts Torg across the train station, and start Nordic walking in Ystad.

(Ystad Tourist Centre phone: 0411-57 76 81; e-mail: turistinfo@ystad.se.)

A Nordic Walk in the City

Location: Ystad's historic downtown

Start to finish: Start at the train station. Stay on the sidewalks. Head west on Österleden and make a right on Hamngatan. As you arrive at the Stora Torget (main square), make a left and stay on the left-hand side but head toward the church, S:ta Maria Kyrkan. Pass the church and continue straight on Stora Väster-gatan. Along this street you should be able to see glimpses of the harbor to

The Krukmakeriet in downtown Ystad.

your left as you cross some smaller streets. At the end of Stora Västergatan, make a right and head into the park, Norra Promenaden. Remove the paws since you will be Nordic walking on dirt. Make another right as you enter the park, and continue straight until you see a restaurant to your left. This is your landmark to exit the park to the *right* on Planteringsgatan. Put the paws back on since you are back on asphalt. Continue straight, but veer soon slightly left onto Lilla Västergatan, which will take you back to the church, S:ta Maria Kyrkan. This time you will make a left by the church to pass the entrance. After the church, make a right and walk along the church. Continue past the main square (Stortorget) and feel the cobblestones under your feet. At the end of the square, make a left. On your right you will pass an old house (Krukmakeriet) where they make pottery. Veer to the left up a tiny hill on Klostergatan, and soon you will pass one of Sweden's best-preserved monasteries on your right, Gråbrödrarklostret, which was built in 1267! Make a right on Hospitalsgatan and walk to the end of the street. Make a right onto a path that will take you past a pond. Keep walking straight on this path, crossing two smaller streets. At the end you will arrive at Stora Östergatan, where you make a right and then an immediate left on Hamngatan to walk back to the train station.

Estimated distance and time: 2 miles (3.2 km), 30 minutes

Difficulty level: Easy

Terrain: Flat

Surface: Asphalt, some cobblestones, some dirt

A Nordic Walk on a Sandy Beach

Location: Ystad Sandskog (Sand Forest of Ystad)

Start to finish: Start the walk by Hotel Ystad Saltsjöbaden and head east. You can make the walk difficult by walking on the sandy beach or easy by staying on the path that runs along the beach, called Badstigen. Both walkers and bikers are allowed on the path (asphalt). After 10 to 15 minutes, the path veers left and ends up by a miniature golf place. Make a right, passing the miniature golf to your left, and continue on Badstigen, which changes

Ystad Sandskog and beach.

surface to compact dirt. The walk takes you into the forest, but you are still walking parallel to the coast. Unless you decided to walk on the beach, you can see the sea only intermittently, but the forest is magical too. At the end of Badstigen you will end up at a place called Nybroån (Newbridge Creek). There are no signs, but you will know it is the end because the path stops after a brisk 45-minute walk. To your right you will find the only house in sight, and to your left there is a parking lot. Turn around and walk back to the hotel. If you wish to visit the beach, make a left after 1 to 2 minutes to head down toward the sea. Maybe you'll decide to walk back on the beach?

If you walked on the beach the whole time, it is easy to know when to turn around: when the sandy beach stops and continues on the other side of a small bay.

Estimated distance and time: 6.2 miles (10 km), 1.5 to 2 hours

Difficulty level: Easy to difficult

Terrain: Flat

Surface: Asphalt, dirt, and sand

Driving and biking directions from the city: From the train station in Ystad located on Österleden, travel east on Österleden. After less than 1 mile (1.5 km) approaching Sand Skogen (the Sand Forest), make a right on Saltsjöbad vägen. Crossing the railroad tracks, you are now traveling south toward the coast. As the road curves to the right, you will see a glimpse of the hotel straight ahead of you. On bike, continue straight ahead. If you drive, continue veering to the right and make an immediate left into the parking lot of the hotel, Ystad Saltsjöbaden. It is a 5- to 10-minute car or bike ride.

Other information and tips: The walk is easy if you stay on the path (asphalt and dirt), but it can become difficult if you choose to walk on the beach itself (soft sand). Visit the Web site for Hotel Ystad Saltsjöbaden at www.ystadssaltsjobad.se.

A Nordic Hike in the Local "Mountains"

Location: Ales Stenar, Kåseberga (Swedish Stonehenge!)

Start to finish: After you park, follow the sign to Ales Stenar, a stone-setting in the form of a ship from the Viking era. The path up to this site is easy to follow if you keep an eye out for the signs saying Ales Stenar. After about 10 minutes at the top of the hill, you will cross another path saying Ahls rökeri to the left. For now, stay on the course to Ales Stenar, but on your return head down

The Swedish Stonehenge: Ales Stenar in Kåseberga.

to Ahls rökeri and Kåseberga harbor for some fresh fish and more hills. It's less than a 5-minute walk down.

Once at the ship barrow, walk inside the stone-setting and continue on a smaller path after the last stone toward the fence. If you want to keep the walk to 30 minutes, return. If you want to enjoy the view some more, walk around on the top of the hill, which provides a flat and grassy surface. Just watch your step since there are no real paths to follow. There are fenced-off areas for cows, but explore safely and respectfully. For a very challenging experience, make a left by the fence and head toward the crest of the ridge.

Continue down on the very steep and sandy hill to the sea. At the bottom make a left and head back up on the path parallel to the one you came down. If the sand gets too challenging, try the grass on the sides. There is only one specific path that will take you from and to the parking. The rest is up to you to explore, but do remember to visit the Kåseberga harbor on your return.

Estimated distance and time: 2 miles (3.2 km), 30 minutes

Difficulty level: Easy to moderate; seaside hills difficult

Elevation: 128 feet (39 m)

Terrain: Hilly and flat

Surface: Dirt, sand, and grass

Driving directions from the city: From the train station in Ystad, travel east on Österleden, passing Sand Skogen. After about 6 miles (9.6 km), as you leave the village of Nybrostrand and the forest ends, get ready to make a right toward Kåseberga to continue traveling along the coast. After about 4.7 miles (7.5 km), make another right to Kåseberga and Ales Stenar. Now you are heading down toward the sea. Take an immediate right into the parking lot. Park and walk toward the beginning of the path toward Ales Stenar. The drive takes about 15 to 20 minutes from Ystad train station.

Other information and tips: Skåne, the province in the south of Sweden, is known for being flat, and in Swedish it is sometimes called "flat as a pancake." However, many areas have beautiful rolling hills, and just 20 minutes outside Ystad by the coast lies a small fishing village (Kåseberga) that offers some hilly nature, historic monument (Ales Stenar), freshly smoked herring, and a beautiful view of the Baltic Sea. It is very windy and thus a perfect location for wind gliders. The Vikings thought it was a perfect location for Ales Stenar, Sweden's largest ship barrow.

The Nordic walks were created by Malin Svensson, Ystad, Sweden (hometown of the author).

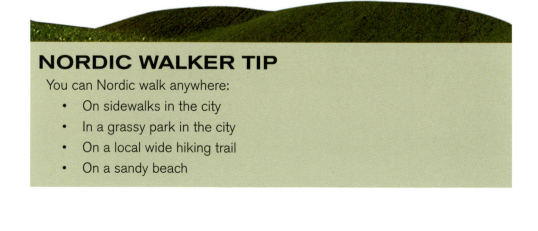

NORDIC WALKER TIP

You can Nordic walk anywhere:

- On sidewalks in the city
- In a grassy park in the city
- On a local wide hiking trail
- On a sandy beach

Designated Nordic Walking Parks

Before Nordic walking was developed, other Nordic sports already existed. As Nordic walking grew, those sports were either modified or new ones were created. This resulted in a wide variety of activities that can be practiced year-round. The menu of choices also allowed anyone at any fitness level or age to find at least one activity they can enjoy. In addition to Nordic walking, Nordic hiking and Nordic blading (in-line skating with poles) can be performed during the dry season. Nordic winter walking (Nordic walking on compact snow), Nordic snowshoeing (snowshoeing with poles), and Nordic fitness skiing (cross-country skiing with wider and shorter skis, still with two styles: classic and skating) can be performed when the snow arrives. Now imagine having access to all those activities during all four seasons in one area. That's what you can find in a Nordic fitness sports park (see www.nordic-fitness-park.de) and other similar places. Some cities even have them designed to fit inside the city, such as Helsinki, Finland. Others have placed the parks outside the cities. Some parks also allow other sports than Nordic sports, such as mountain biking. The common thing is that you can arrive, look at a billboard, and check what route you want to Nordic walk. There are various lengths and difficulty levels, and all routes are well marked by signs so you can't get lost. Some parks also offer rental of equipment including instructions. Basically, it is like going to a gym—an outdoor gym—where you have numerous activities to choose from.

Conclusion

Now that you know you can go Nordic walking anywhere around your city—on sidewalks, in a grassy park, on the beach, or on a wide hiking trail—and basically anywhere in the world, the rest is up to you to explore. Explore your own city, a new city, and maybe even a new country. Not comfortable traveling by yourself? Travel in a group or vacation at a Nordic walking destination. (See appendix B for more resources.) Browse the Internet to discover and dream about new places and things to do, but actually traveling to experience the world is a memory for life.

CHAPTER 5

Outdoor Safety and Etiquette

We do not inherit the land from our ancestors; we borrow it from our children.

Native American proverb

Are you a city lover, enjoying the action? Or are you a country person, loving the simplicity and peacefulness of nature? Maybe you're a little bit of both. In either case, you have to be prepared before you step into the specific environment. It's like planning for a trip: You need to pack your bathing suit if you are going to a warm climate to relax in the sun by the pool, lake, or ocean. And you need to pack the warm jacket that will keep you comfortable in a cold paradise. On the trail in the mountains, you will most likely not find any conveniently located shops when you get thirsty or hungry or get a blister on your hand or foot. Before you head out, you need to think about bringing those necessary items. If you are not accustomed to being outdoors, you may be hesitant to try it. A good start for a true city person is a local trail that is flat or just slightly hilly. Once you get used to it, you will love what the outdoors has to offer. As mentioned in chapter 4, the best way to discover a new city is to have a local person show you around. The same thing applies to outside the city limits in nature. Maybe in your circle of friends there is an avid hiker who can introduce you to an easy and enjoyable trail. Just as there are rules in the city to prevent traffic accidents, there are rules in nature—just not always made by humans. Learn as much as possible about the area you're going to so you can safely interact with nature. When you go Nordic walking in the city, you will also be outdoors but in a different environment that requires a different type of preparation.

This chapter offers advice on personal safety as well as on safely handling the poles. There is advice specifically for Nordic walking in the city and specifically for Nordic walking (hiking) in the mountains. This book focuses on local mountains that offer marked trails that take anywhere from one to three hours to finish. Whether you are a pedestrian in the city or a hiker in the mountains, there are certain things to be aware of to keep everyone happy. This chapter provides reminders on taking responsibility for your own health when exercising while maintaining respect for the health of the earth.

Personal Safety

To be as safe as possible outdoors, you must take a few things into consideration: the condition of your health, the items you bring, how much water and food you pack, how you dress for the weather, and how you act and react in the city as well as in the mountains.

Health Status

Before starting any exercise regimen, consult with your doctor. Make sure you are in good health to Nordic walk a certain distance at a certain intensity. Get clearance from the doctor before hitting the streets or trails. This is for your own safety as well as for anyone working out with you. Exercising should be good for you, not harmful. However, there are risks, including heart stress and musculoskeletal injuries, when you take your body to another level.

It may have been years since you exercised, and you may think you can start up where you left off. That's not a good idea. You lose what you don't use. Be wise and start with a level your body will be able to handle today. A good rule is to set yourself up for victory, not for failure. If you start out too hard, not only do you risk becoming injured, but you also risk losing interest in sticking to the new exercise program. So ease into it. The great thing about exercising is that it creates muscle memory. If you were accustomed to a lot of physical activity years ago, your body will most likely remember and make progress just fine. If you have never physically exerted yourself, then take one step at a time and listen carefully to your body. If anything hurts, stop. Try to distinguish between various feelings of discomfort. If it is a feeling of fatigue, most likely you are all right. But if it is a feeling of pain, you need to stop what you're doing. Exercising on a regular basis will benefit you, but not overnight. Be patient and gradually build to the next fitness level. Feeling bad about being in bad shape is not going to get you into shape. Actually, it may stop you from trying. Turn it around and use it as a point of reference. Choose Nordic walking up a hill or a route that is tough today. Compare in a month and check the difference. If you've been working out consistently, you should feel a difference. That's progress. The key now is to maintain what you have and maybe continue to build to the next fitness goal. Always compare your fitness status to your individual situation and not to anyone else's.

Weather

The walks presented in this book include city walks, city park walks, and marked trail hikes. It is a good idea to check the weather reports before heading out. Change in weather is always an issue, especially if you choose a more isolated walk or hike. Check the weather also so that you can dress appropriately. The more prepared you are, the more enjoyable the experience will be.

Just-in-Case Items

Even if you head out for a 30-minute Nordic walk, you would want to bring some items that will aid you in case something were to happen on your walk. When you purchase a water belt, make sure you get one that has a pouch that's big enough to carry the following items: a fully charged cell phone, a current ID, a note with contact information to three local people in case of an emergency, some cash, and a valid credit card.

Food and Water

The amount of food and water to consume during your Nordic walk depends on your individual needs, the intensity and duration of the Nordic walk, and the weather conditions. If you have a specific medical condition such as diabetes, you need to determine what and how much you should bring. The higher the intensity and the longer the duration of the aerobic workout, the greater

Everywhere is walking distance if you have the time.

Steven Wright

the amount of water loss. It's the body's way of preventing overheating. The water loss is mainly through sweating. If the weather is hot, your water loss will be even greater.

By the time you feel thirsty, your body has already been in need of water for some time. That's why it's important to drink on a regular basis. At rest, there seems to be a balance between the water intake and the water loss. As you start exercising, water loss increases. Water regulates the body temperature. As you exercise, the demand on muscle work increases. The muscles in the body need to produce energy to work. In this energy production, heat is a by-product. Thus body temperature increases as you exercise. To prevent overheating, the blood transports the heat to the skin where it evaporates—in other words, you sweat.

When you exercise in hot temperatures, the muscles and the skin fight over the blood distribution. The muscles need the blood to deliver oxygen to keep going. The skin needs the blood to transport the heat so it can evaporate to keep the body cool.

About 50 to 60 percent of a young person's body weight is water. A water loss of only 9 to 12 percent of a person's total body weight can be fatal. Dehydration has an increased stress effect (unhealthy increase in heart rate and body temperature) on the cardiovascular system. The volume of the blood will decrease since blood consists of water. A decrease in blood volume means a decrease in blood pressure. This means that less blood will reach the muscles and skin. Decreased blood to the skin to let the heat out means the body temperature increases. To compensate for the negative impact of dehydration, the body has to increase the heart rate to try to pump out more blood. Thus a dehydrated athlete's performance will be compromised.

Drink before, during, and after exercise. The American College of Sports Medicine (ACSM) recommends drinking 16 ounces (about half a liter) of fluid 2 hours before exercise. During exercise, drink 6 to 12 ounces (about 180-360 ml) of chilled water every 15 to 20 minutes. Estimate your time for your Nordic walk so you will bring enough water. Since weight loss after an aerobic session is mainly caused by water loss, you can weigh yourself before and after the exercise to make sure you replace the fluid. For every pound (about half a kilogram) lost, drink 16 ounces (480 ml) of fluid.

If you exercise for less than 60 minutes in one bout, drinking water should be enough. If you exercise for longer than 60 minutes in one bout, you will benefit from adding an electrolyte-replacement beverage (which contains sodium, potassium, and calcium). Athletes who exercise nonstop for more than 3 hours should be aware of a medical condition called hyponatremia. It is caused by drinking *too much fluid,* which can cause an imbalance in the body's fluid and sodium levels. The sodium levels get too low, and the symptoms can be nausea, vomiting, headache, and in general not feeling well. If it gets worse, the symptoms can include confusion, delayed reactions, seizure, disorientation, and even coma.

Several factors can influence the body's performance during endurance training. Dehydration and depletion of carbohydrate can both result in muscle fatigue and thus poor performance. Just as your car needs fuel in order to operate, your body needs food in order to function. The separate nutrients in food (carbohydrate, fat, protein, vitamins, minerals, and water) have distinct purposes for the body to function properly. Carbohydrate, found in grains, vegetables, and fruit, is the body's main source of energy during exercise. It has to be broken down into glucose so the muscle cells can easily use it for energy production. Whatever glucose is not used gets stored. Stored glucose is called glycogen. Glycogen is stored in the liver and the skeletal muscles.

If you are physically active, then 60 to 65 percent of the calories you consume should come from carbohydrate. If you work out vigorously for more than an hour nonstop, you may need to add some easily absorbed carbohydrate, like glucose (high concentration in grapes, figs, sweet fruits, and honey), during exercise to delay muscle fatigue. To make it more convenient to add during the workout, you can add a glucose solution to your drink, or try a good sport drink. There is a powder called Carbo Plus from Universal Nutrition. Power Bar comes in a bar but also conveniently in a gel form in a pouch, or try a good old Gatorade sport drink. There are a myriad of products and brands and sometimes it is best to just try them out to see what works best for you. Make sure it is a mixture of glucose and fructose and you might just as well make sure it contains electrolytes. For longer Nordic walks or hikes, bring a snack, such as a sport bar or trail mix. A trained person has the ability to store more glycogen and thus deplete the glycogen during exercise at a slower rate, resulting in the ability to keep going longer. Within two hours of your workout is the best time to replenish the glycogen storage. According to some sources, a combination of carbohydrate and protein is ideal (4 grams of carbohydrate for every 1 gram of protein) for speeding the recovery.

City Streets and Traffic

In some cities you see very few people walking around because of safety, accessibility, or lack of scenery, basically because the city does not offer a walking friendly environment. Next time you are in a city, observe *where* you see most pedestrians. The global direction toward inactivity creates not only direct health problems such as obesity, but also concern for the health of the planet. More driving equals less physical movement. More cars also equal more carbon dioxide (CO_2) emission, a threat to everything and everyone living on earth. It is unhealthy to walk outdoors in some cities because of air pollution. For a long time, city planners have been aware of numerous problems with the infrastructure in newer cities. Continuing to build suburbs with no direct communication with nearby cities is a long-term disaster. There is a need for refocusing on urban living—that is, working and living in the same area as well as improving mass transit systems. Creating more walking- and biking-friendly communities is another step in the right direction: It will be safer and more accessible for pedestrians, and it will be a more enjoyable experience walking in an environment that is pleasing to the eye. Compare walking along a noisy, wide road with high speed limits to walking on a narrower road with slower speed limits and beautiful architecture and landscaping. All the indirect and positive side effects will automatically increase people's physical activity. If you use your body more for transportation and rely less on the car, then you contribute to creating a healthier future for coming generations.

As you get out Nordic walking on a sidewalk in the city, be street smart (see figure 5.1). Although talking to a walking buddy, listening to music, and talking on a cell phone are great motivational tools to keep you exercising, they can also be negative distractions in traffic. Be especially attentive as you cross a street even if you have the right of way. In some cultures it is common to make a right turn (if it's safe) against a red light. As a pedestrian, always be one step ahead of what every car is about to do. The cautious crossing applies to all crossings, whether it is a street with cars or a path designated for bikers and in-line skaters. If you walk in an unfamiliar city, always ask somebody at the hotel (or somebody trustworthy) what areas to avoid for safety reasons.

Figure 5.1 (*a*) A street that is not inviting for walking, and (*b*) a street that is inviting for walking.

WALKING-FRIENDLY COMMUNITIES: SMALL TO LARGE

Run the Planet picked the top five U.S. cities in three population categories as the most walkable communities. To be selected, the cities needed to provide compact and diverse development, places to walk, no impassable barriers, beauty, and safety.

Small

1. Dunedin, Florida
2. Exeter, New Hampshire
3. Eureka Springs, Arkansas
4. Burlington, Vermont
5. Xenia, Ohio

Medium

1. Boulder, Colorado
2. Chattanooga, Tennessee
3. Raleigh, North Carolina
4. Portland, Maine
5. Austin, Texas

Large

1. Washington, DC
2. Minneapolis, Minnesota
3. Boston, Massachusetts
4. Portland, Oregon
5. Seattle and Kirkland, Washington

Run the Planet (www.runtheplanet.com/trainingracing/training/walkers/americancities.asp).

Ask what areas they recommend for walkers. Otherwise you may miss that beautiful walk just around the corner. Also ask what time the sun sets so you can plan to be back before dark. Bring a city map and make sure you mark the starting point before you head out on your adventure.

Trail

When you leave the city limits and step into nature, you enter a domain where humans do not create all the rules. Remember this and prepare for the specific area you are about to enter. Find out if there are some typical insects, plants, or

SAFETY TIP

Paws off on trails, grass, sand, snow, and icy parts.

wildlife you should be aware of. Pack your first aid kit based on the information. One common insect is the mosquito. If you find out ahead of time that there are lots of mosquitoes, you can easily bring a repellent in your first aid kit and make your life easier. If there is a poisonous plant that is common on the trail, find out what it looks like for the specific season and how to treat your skin if you were to touch it by accident. Add that ointment to your first aid kit. Basically, customize your first aid kit based on the environment for the specific hikes you choose.

Walking with a blister for five minutes may be painful but doable. When you get into one- to three-hour walks, it is far from paradise. Use good socks and good shoes of the correct size and shape to avoid friction, which causes blisters. If the shoes are new, you may want to gradually break them in on several shorter walks and wait for that three-hour hike until they are completely comfortable. Another preventive trick is to apply petroleum jelly to your feet before putting on the socks. Make sure you carry a doughnut-shaped moleskin pad in your first aid kit. If you were to still get a blister and you can't stop walking, apply the moleskin and keep the area of the blister open. Otherwise stop walking and change shoes. The goal is to prevent the blister from getting bigger. If it is a bigger blister (larger than 1 inch, or 2.5 cm), drain it. Refer to the Internet for easy instructions. A blister can get infected and then medical attention would be necessary. Pack other useful typical first aid items for treating wounds, ankle sprains, and stings. Include waterproof matches, a needle, sterile bandage, antibiotic ointment, and eye irritant solution. Add a pencil and a notepad as well.

The Nordic walks (hikes) featured here are on marked trails that take no longer than three hours. The more isolated the routes, the more vulnerable you are unless you are an experienced wilderness hiker. Make sure you always walk with someone and that you report the route to a ranger or somebody in charge of the park. If there is no such person, then place a note on your car and describe the route you are about to head out on. Include time and date of your departure, estimated time of arrival, and contact information to somebody locally.

On a three-hour marked trail, you can run into hunters, mountain bikers, horses, dogs, snakes, bears, and other wildlife. Never threaten any animal; of course it is best to just avoid them. Make noise as you hike, and walk in groups with small children in the middle. On an encounter, make yourself as big as possible by using the poles, and slowly back away. If you turn around to sprint, you could be interpreted as prey, and the animal may chase you.

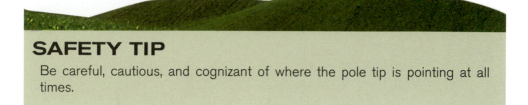

SAFETY TIP

Be careful, cautious, and cognizant of where the pole tip is pointing at all times.

To avoid hunters, hike only in areas where hunting is restricted. If you run into riders on horses, give them plenty of space. Be still and quiet, and don't make any sudden movements. Avoid doing anything that could spook them. Never try to touch a horse unless the rider agrees.

Many trails allow mountain bikers. Find out ahead of time so you are prepared for what may come fast and uncontrollably around the corner. Dogs may run around without a leash. If they are protective of their owners, do not approach them unless you get permission from the owners. Even then, practice common sense. The Nordic walking poles can be useful as protection. If it's legal in your country, bring some kind of animal mace or pepper spray.

Pole Safety

When I teach Nordic walking to beginners, I emphasize how to handle the poles safely. Before you get accustomed to the poles, you might move them around awkwardly in such a way that you could end up poking your walking partner or an innocent passer-by. Be especially careful when the spike tip is exposed (see figure 5.2). Nordic walking in a group is great fun; you just need to watch where you place your poles and your feet. Fortunately, you can walk and talk and still stay safe—it all becomes second nature after a very short while.

Figure 5.2 An exposed spike tip can be sharp.

The poles feel different on different terrain. Practice makes master—the more you change surfaces and terrain, the better you will get to know your Nordic walking poles.

Exposed Spike Tip

When you remove the asphalt paws, make sure you do it on one pole at a time while the other pole is safely on the ground. Remove the paw of the pole you are holding. If it's a new pole, it's easier to turn it upside down with the grip facing down into the ground. If the pole has a basket (part of the whole spike tip piece), hold on to the basket (otherwise it may come off as well) with your left hand while you wiggle the paw off with your right hand. If it is not a new pole, grab the paw with your dominant hand. Place the other hand in the center of the pole. Hold the pole horizontally in front of you. Unscrew the paw by turning the dominant hand on the paw one way and the other hand in the opposite direction. Basically, twist the paw off. Place the pole on the ground and then put the paw in your pocket. Pick up the second pole from the ground to remove its paw. Repeat the same procedure with the other pole. Place it on the ground and put away the paw. With both paws in your pocket, pick up both poles by the grips so that the spike tips are facing down. With exposed spike tips, always keep the poles in a vertical position.

Nordic Walking With Two or More People

Whether you get warmed up (*before* Nordic walking) or stretched out (*after* Nordic walking) by performing the dynamic exercises and static stretches in this book with a group of people, you want to keep the asphalt paws on at all times as well as keep a distance of more than one length of a pole in between each other. When you begin the Nordic walking portion of your workout, as part of a group, you could easily step on the person's pole in front of you. Maintain a distance greater than both your poles together. Stepping on a person's paw can yank his shoulder back as he continues moving forward, causing pain and maybe even an injury in the shoulder joint.

Also keep a safe distance between you and the person walking next to you. You may trip over your partner's poles. The result may be amusing for those around you, but not necessarily to you, especially if you actually do fall and get hurt. At the very least, your ego will be bruised, if not your knees.

SAFETY TIP

Always store poles with the paws on. Store them horizontally so they can't fall or, if they are leaning on a wall, make sure the paws are on the floor.

Pole Safety in Various Terrains and Surfaces

When Nordic hiking, look 6 to 10 feet (2 to 3 m) in front of you to make sure you avoid planting your pole in a hole. Planting a pole in a hole can cause you to lose your footing, or if it gets stuck and you don't realize it, it could pull your shoulder back sharply on your next stride. In rocky areas, the poles have a tendency to have a life of their own by bouncing around a little. It is highly recommended to keep extra distance behind a Nordic hiker since the paws will be off. The sharp pole tip could bounce off a slippery rock's surface, or the person in front of you may slip, causing her to flail and send her pole straight back toward you. So keep a safe distance on the rocks. While going uphill with exposed spike tips, keep a good distance from the person ahead of you. You never know when and if that person may slip with the pole—regardless of whether that person is a beginner or a seasoned Nordic walker. In the winter, you can slip with the poles on the icy parts even while walking on terrain. Again, keep a safe distance from the person in front of you. When walking on grass and crossing a short stretch of asphalt, it can be tempting to lift the poles off the ground to keep the noise down. Although it's fine for the metal of the spike tip to be used temporarily on asphalt, it may be too noisy. If you lift the poles off the ground, ensure that the spike tips are pointing down. You can do this by keeping the poles vertical. If you keep swinging the poles off the ground, you may end up poking somebody behind you. While learning Nordic walking (part II), you will actually be encouraged to keep walking through *short* stretches of asphalt with spike tips exposed to test that you're not dragging the poles but instead planting them once for every step you take.

Practicing Outdoor Etiquette and Ethics

Nordic walking is a relatively new sport and fitness exercise, so people may get very distracted when they see you Nordic walking. This is both good and bad. It is good because you'll get noticed and thus the word about this new

TECHNIQUE TIP

If you are part of a group that Nordic walks together, keep more than a pole's distance between you and the walker in front of you. If you end up accidentally stepping on the person's pole while it's extended behind him, the abrupt pull can strain a muscle or cause a shoulder injury.

great activity will spread further. It is bad if somebody gets so distracted that she forgets about her own walking. One time a driver got so distracted by a huge Nordic walking group in a park that he ran into a tree. The driver was not hurt, just immensely embarrassed.

Make your Nordic walking experience an enjoyable one. Practice good etiquette while meeting other people in the city or in the mountains, and be respectful to the city, nature, and wildlife.

Pedestrians and Hikers

As you are Nordic walking in the city, give the right of way to other people you meet on the sidewalk. The list includes other people exercising: walkers, joggers, and runners. If there is more than one Nordic walker, make sure you get into a single file when the sidewalk or path gets narrow. It is likely that you will run into trekkers and other Nordic walkers and hikers on the trails. Practice good etiquette and avoid crowding people. Use common sense.

Nature

Whether you are in nature, in the city, or anywhere else, *never* litter. It is depressing to see trash in beautiful nature. There may not be a trash can conveniently located when you need one. Always bring a plastic bag for waste disposal on

Be responsible—clean up!

Nature the way it's supposed to look.

trails and on longer and isolated routes. In a worst-case scenario, take trash home to throw away. Just as you need to take care of your own health, you need to take care of the health of Mother Earth. If you see trash that doesn't belong to you, it is of course good practice to pick it up. Kids walking with you will pick up those good habits. Leave plants, branches, and flowers where they belong—in nature. Don't bring anything home with you, unless it has fallen down. Let the people who come behind you experience the beauty you just experienced. Leave everything the way you found it. Be respectful of both nature and the wildlife.

Wildlife

As mentioned in the beginning of this chapter, you are entering land that belongs to the wildlife. In many areas, houses are being built closer and closer to the wildlife. Yet people get very upset when reading about a mountain lion getting inside people's yards and maybe even killing a dear pet of the family. Although it is horrible, no doubt about it, you have to understand that you are moving into the domain of the mountain lion. One mountain lion needs anywhere from 15 to 35 square miles (24-56 square km) depending on the sex, the habitat, and the level of difficulty of finding food.

Conclusion

Some things are taken for granted in life. One may be that Mother Earth will always be here for humans. Who knows what lies ahead, but everyone can agree on one thing: If your children and grandchildren are going to enjoy this planet as much as you have, you'd better start taking care of it. Whether you Nordic walk in the city, in a park, or on a mountain trail, respect the people you meet and, above all, respect nature and wildlife. This chapter prepares you to have a safe and enjoyable walk that you can share with generations to come.

10 Essentials for the Nordic Walker's Safety

- ☐ Nordic walking poles
- ☐ Nordic walking shoes and good socks
- ☐ Heart rate monitor
- ☐ Appropriate clothing for the weather
- ☐ Familiarity with the route
- ☐ Walking partner
- ☐ Water belt with a pouch
- ☐ Cell phone, ID, some cash, a credit card
- ☐ Snack, such as a sport bar or nuts
- ☐ First aid kit and waste disposal on longer or isolated walks

Nordic Walking Techniques and Workouts

CHAPTER 6

Basic Nordic Walking

The roots of education are bitter, but the fruit is sweet.

Aristotle

There is a big difference between learning to use Nordic walking poles *with instructions* and learning to use them *without instructions*. This applies both to strapping into the poles (unless they are strapless) and using them. Very often people start using them as feet and legs. As you land with your feet, you land first with the heel in front of your body and then roll onto the rest of the foot to push off from the ball of the foot behind your body to land again in front of your body. If you do the same with the pole—landing with the asphalt paw or spike tip in front of the body—you will put on the brakes. Maybe you will receive some support and balance, but you will not reap the benefits of burning more calories and strengthening the upper body. The purpose of planting the pole in an angle behind the body is to propel the body forward, not to push on the brakes. Unless you are a cross-country skier or you have received some instruction in Nordic walking, you will not figure it out. Save the trouble of trial and error and follow the simple instructions in this chapter on using your Nordic walking poles correctly.

Since Nordic walking is an enhancement of regular walking, this chapter starts with reviewing how to walk correctly without the poles. Even though walking may be a natural way for you to move, you will have some new things to think about while walking. This memory process and application will be easier if you leave the poles behind for now. The fewer distractions there are, the better you can concentrate. Then add the poles and you will be way ahead of the game as you learn the basics and the other intensifiers of Nordic walking. Basic Nordic walking is a place you can return to even when you are at more advanced levels. As with anything, a solid foundation is crucial before you make any additions. Too often people rush into learning everything at once, and the second another add-on or intensifier is mentioned, the basics are out the window. This will be all right if you are isolating the move to work on it for a while. However, as you integrate it into your Nordic walking technique, make sure you have a solid foundation. Even on your first day of Nordic walking, it is good to practice up- and downhill, especially if you live in hilly areas. Hill training will not only get you into great shape faster, but it also teaches you upfront how to use the poles. It is actually easier to climb than to descend with the poles. If you know the downhill technique, it will save your joints with or

NORDIC WALKER TIP

Any of the techniques or levels can be used on any surface in any environment. For example, you can perform Level 2 and Level 3 on a sidewalk in the city. You don't have to find a grassy park or a local trail.

without your poles. The main focus is on changing the body position and the weight distribution instead of changing the height of the poles.

Basic Regular Walking Technique

As mentioned previously, Nordic walking is an enhancement of regular walking. Check how you currently walk (see figure 6.1). People look at me amusingly when I tell them I am going to observe their walks. If there are some incorrect patterns, they laugh when I tell them I will help them correct it. Every person who is able to walk thinks he or she can walk. Yes, a person can go from point A to point B. But how efficient and how pain free is that walk? When your foot lands, it has so many options to move (or not move) due to muscle strength and flexibility in the whole body. When you apply all your body weight on that poor foot seconds later, your ankle joint had better get all the support it needs from the correct muscles to carry your weight.

Clients stop laughing, especially if aches and pains disappear, as they rediscover their bodies and become aware of how they walk. Practice one step at a

The longest journey begins with a single step.

Lao-tzu

Figure 6.1 Walking correctly.

time as you walk around indoors or outdoors. See how it feels, and be aware of it next time you go for a stroll.

1. Heel Strikes First

When you land with the foot, you want to make sure you land with the heel first, more specifically with the *center of the heel* first. Walk around and see if it feels as though you are doing it that way. Focus on one foot at a time.

2. Rock and Roll Like a Rocker

After you land with the heel, continue to roll onto the rest of the foot. You can practice this rolling movement by first standing still: Rock back and forth from heel to toes like a rocking chair. It is fairly easy to hear feet that don't roll, especially with shoes on when you're going downhill. There is a slapping sound. Feet that roll are almost soundless. Try it and listen. Next time you have shoes on while walking down a hill, listen and decide whether your feet are slapping or are quiet. If you are prone to sore shins, the slapping of the feet could be one cause.

Note: Avoid the *arch collapse*. Though there is a slight pronation (rolling inward) during the landing of the foot, the arch should not roll in too much or collapse. You need to have a strong foundation to land on in order to hold up the rest of the body. If the arch collapses, maybe the knee and the hip will follow. If untreated, this instability through the joints each time you take a step can eventually lead to injuries.

3. Heel Comes Off the Ground

As you roll onto the ball of the foot (base of the toes), the heel comes off the ground. If you previously did the rocking-back-and-forth movement, you may have experienced the sensation. Now walk around and feel the heel coming off. Concentrate on one foot only.

4. Push Off With the Ball of the Foot

Then push the ball of the foot down and back into the ground. This push-off action propels the body forward. Walk around and feel how you push off with the base of the toes.

Note: To be more precise with the location of the push-off, it's easier if you sit down to find it on one foot. Cross your left leg and let the left foot rest on top of the right knee. With your right hand, grab all toes on the left foot. Then move the hand farther down to the base of the toes (ball of the foot). Move to the base of the big toe and the second toe. Mark (in your mind) that location with an X. This is the precise location of the push-off. Walk around again, this time practicing the push-off from the X location.

5. Activate the Buttocks

At the same time you push off with the ball of the foot, you activate the very bottom of the buttock! That is singular. Tighten only one buttock. Feel the connection between push-off action of the ball of the foot and the activation of the buttock of the same leg.

6. Fall (Lean) Forward

As you walk, make sure you lean forward as one unit. It feels almost as if you are falling forward. The weight should be on the balls of the feet. Always keep that core activated in a neutral pelvic position to avoid any bending in the waist or rounding of the back as you lean forward. Walk around and see how it feels to lean forward as one unit. Does it feel as if you are increasing your speed? If so, you are doing it correctly.

7. Arm Meets Opposite Leg

Start walking. After a few steps, glance down so you can see your left arm swinging forward. Next, observe what foot lands at the same time. Yes, the right foot lands at the same time the left arm swings forward. Basically, left arm meets right leg, and right arm meets left leg. This is the natural walking rhythm, and most people don't even think about it—it just happens naturally. If you can't see it, exaggerate the arm swings to match the pace of the legs. If it gets you out of rhythm, then shake it off and start walking again. Have somebody observe your arm and leg movement instead.

8. Use an Even and Straight Arm Swing

When you have the arm and leg rhythm down, make sure the arm swing is *even*. In other words, you swing the arm as much forward as you swing it backward. This is hard to see on yourself unless somebody videotapes you from the side. One solution is to stand sideways in front of a mirror. Swing one arm and see if you have an even swing or if it mainly swings forward. Try to correct it and walk around with this awareness.

Note: Also make sure that the arms swing straight forward and back. Avoid rotational arm movement, especially when you add a slight rotation of the torso (step 9). Don't cross the arms in front of you. Keep them moving straight forward and back.

9. Slightly Twist the Rib Cage

Stand still and place your hands around the rib cage (see figure 6.2*a*), just below the chest. Keep your head and hips straight as you softly turn the rib cage from right (see figure 6.2*b*) to left. Feel the twist (rotation). Focus on the solar plexus, where the axis of the rotation takes place. Try maintaining this twisting movement as you release the hands (see figure 6.2*c*). Start walking and add this slight rotation to your walk. Don't slow down, but keep a regular pace. A slight torso rotation to the *left* naturally moves the *right* arm forward. That also means that the opposite leg, in this case the *left* one, moves forward. Remember step 7: Arm meets opposite leg.

Note: This soft upper-body rotation matches the lower-body rotation. The upper-body rotation results in movement of the shoulders, and the lower-body rotation results in movement of the hips. A common mistake is to move the shoulders by themselves without initiating the slight rotation. The initiation of the rotation is in the axis. This means that if you focus on initiating the

Figure 6.2 *(a)* Hands around rib cage; *(b)* turn the rib cage in both directions; *(c)* keep turning gently with hands released.

slight rotation in the solar plexus, the shoulders and hips have no choice but to move.

10. Walking in Balance

It is very important that you keep the core activated and the shoulder blades stabilized during the slight rotation. Divide the body into two parts: upper and lower. Their meeting place is in the solar plexus. By *initiating* movement from the inside from this meeting place, you have created an efficient way for the body to maintain balance while walking. By now you should be walking as if you are on top of the world.

Basic Nordic Walking Technique

The basic Nordic walking technique presented in this book is simple so that you can get started right away. There are numerous teaching methods as well as techniques. Once you meet with a certified Nordic walking instructor, trainer, or coach, you will be able to polish your technique. Remember that the better your technique, the more benefits you will see. Appendix B lists Web sites that have information about instructors and resources in your area. The following paragraphs present information to help you learn the basic technique as well as common mistakes and ways of correcting mistakes.

There are various types of Nordic walking poles and almost as many ways of strapping into the poles. Make sure you get proper instruction from the retailer or instructor who sells you the poles or from a DVD if you purchase the poles online. If you decide to begin on asphalt, make sure the asphalt paws are on. The paws should be pointing backward—in other words, the opposite direction of where you are walking. If you decide to start on grass or dirt, the paws should be off. Since the spike tips are exposed when the paws are off, review chapter 5, page 109, for the safe removal of the paws. If you have adjustable poles, now is the time to get them to the correct length. To review the correct length, refer to page 52 in chapter 3. Once you are strapped in snugly and comfortably, you are ready to get started.

Preworkout Checklist of Nordic Walking Poles

☐ Check and adjust length of poles.

☐ Put paws on for asphalt.

☐ Make sure paws face the correct direction (backward).

☐ Take paws off for dirt and grass.

☐ Strap in correctly and comfortably (unless they're strapless poles).

Find the Natural Walking Rhythm

To practice finding the natural walking rhythm, find a big open area that has no obstacles ahead of you (see figure 6.3).

Stand still with poles strapped in. Relax your arms and shoulders. Let the arms just hang heavily at your sides for a while. Open the hands to make them even more relaxed. If you have strapless poles, just barely hold on to the grip. Forget for a moment that you have poles hanging from your hands. Now, start walking as if you were just going for a leisurely stroll. While the poles are dragging on the ground, the arms are swinging to match the leg rhythm. Don't think; just walk.

After about 100 yards or meters of walking this way, glance down at the right arm. Observe it as it swings forward. After a while, check what foot lands as you swing the right arm forward. It should be the left one. *If this is the case, skip the next paragraph.*

If this does not happen naturally for you, don't worry; you are not alone. Stop and destrap and take the poles off. Continue walking without the poles and observe your right arm swinging again and then notice which foot lands simultaneously. Find a way for them to match. One way is to say, "Now," each

Figure 6.3 Find the natural walking rhythm: arm meets opposite leg.

time the right arm swings forward. On each "Now," the left foot should land. Practice this until it feels natural.

Note: The dragging of the poles is just an exercise that allows you to find the natural walking rhythm. It is *not* part of the finished Nordic walking technique. However, it is a great way to start off each Nordic walking workout before the natural walking rhythm becomes automatic.

Plant in a Handshake Position

Once you have the natural walking rhythm, continue observing the *height* of your forward arm swing. If it is at about navel level, you have a sufficiently high forward swing. Keep a good pace. Walk around with this observation (sufficiently high forward swing) for a while. Poles are still dragging, arms and shoulders are still relaxed, and hands are still open.

At the maximum height (navel height) of the forward swing of the arm, you will feel the end of the pole catch the ground. The second you feel that traction, grab the grip of the pole and plant the pole (see figure 6.4). Continue walking around with this new sensation while planting each time at navel height

Figure 6.4 Correct way of planting the pole: Plant at navel height, keep a firm grip using the strap as well, keep the elbow in front of the waist (handshake position), maintain pole angle, and make sure the opposite foot lands at the same time the pole plants.

in a handshake position. You should feel how the arm and other muscles of the upper body are engaged. Make sure you give the grip a good squeeze as you plant the pole. If you only tap, you won't engage as many muscles. Walk around and compare the feelings of planting the pole firmly and barely planting the pole. The great thing about a snugly fit strap is that it should be used to transfer the power. This way your knuckles won't turn white from pressing down on the grip.

If you are able to maintain the angle of the pole, skip this paragraph. Many people change the angle of the pole so that it suddenly plants vertically. This will change the direction of the force. Stop the planting and return to finding the natural walking rhythm you practiced earlier.

Continue observing the position of the elbow as you plant the pole. Is it in front of your body, or is it glued to the waist? *If it is in front so that the whole arm is in a handshake position, skip the rest of this paragraph.* It is very common for people to move only the elbow joint, and it will look like an up-and-down pumping motion. To make more muscles work in your upper body, you want to let the shoulder joint move forward and back. You can practice this by imagining that you shake somebody's hand each time you plant the pole. Check it out while standing sideways in front of a mirror. Are you pretending to shake someone's hand with your elbow glued to your waist? It feels awkward and restrictive. Instead, unglue the elbow from the waist. This will allow the shoulder joint to move. From the side, the upper arm will look like a pendulum swinging back and forth.

To ensure you are not dragging the poles anymore, walk briefly on asphalt without the paws. If you hear a clicking sound once as you plant the pole, you are doing it correctly. If you hear a dragging sound, you are still dragging the poles. You can easily correct this by Nordic walking temporarily without paws on asphalt until you are able to hear only one clicking sound.

Push the Hand Back to the Hip

As you plant the pole, keep applying that firm pressure as you push back and down on the pole (see figure 6.5). This is the action that will propel the body forward, and this is why you plant the pole at an angle and not vertically. You don't want to move up to the sky; you want to move forward. This is the easiest one to describe, but it requires the most of your effort. While some people have strong backs and arms and can thus push farther back, others will have to practice more. It's a good motivation, though, because it will strengthen and shape the back as well as the triceps. Review the strengthening exercises in chapter 2 to prepare for this segment in the Nordic walking technique.

When you feel you have pushed as far back as you can, soften the grip a little before you return to planting the pole again. With a snug strap, it should still feel that you are one with the pole. It should not feel like you are about to lose the pole when you soften the grip. If so, stop to tighten the strap.

It will take some practice to get the coordination of the squeeze as you plant and the slight release at the end of the pushing phase. Once you can maneuver

Figure 6.5 Push the hand back at least to the hip in basic Nordic walking. Soften the grip by the hip.

TECHNIQUE TIP

Here are some key points on gradually building your basic Nordic walking technique:

1. Drag the poles.
2. Match the arm swing with the leg swing.
3. Plant pole firmly (using the strap as well) in a handshake position.
4. Push back to hip.
5. Soften grip by the hip.
6. Return to planting; pole is airborne.
7. Do not drag the poles.

this, your muscles will be very happy. They will go from tension to relaxation. If you walk around with constantly tensed muscles, you will become fatigued and your muscles will be sore. Practice this coordination and your muscles will learn to stay more relaxed.

Climbing and Descending

If you haven't felt the need to add a pair of poles to your regular walking routine, hill training will definitely change your mind. Not only will hill training quickly teach you how to use the poles properly, but the arms will also get amazingly tired. Of course, this depends on the steepness of the hill. A slight incline suitable for a deconditioned person will not be a challenge for a very fit person. The technique, though, is pretty much the same apart from some adjustments, depending on the steepness of the hill.

Nordic Walking Downhill

Apply the basic Nordic walking technique as you go down the hill and think about how you can give your joints a break (see figure 6.6). Don't slow down, unless it hurts—you may have real joint problems. If your joints are healthy, you can still keep a good speed downhill, but take shorter steps at a higher frequency. A regular or longer stride down a steep hill increases the impact on your ankle, knee, and hip joints. Avoid that extra stress. Keep it short and sweet for the joints. Next, bend your knees and make sure you keep landing on the heel and rolling onto the rest of the foot. No push-off is possible going downhill. This should all be familiar to you if you practiced the basics in regular walking in the beginning of this chapter. The steeper the hill, the more you bend your knees. As you bend, the knees should stay behind the toes to avoid additional pressure on the knees.

Figure 6.6 Adjusting the body and adding support from the poles will decrease the stress on the joints while you're going downhill.

TECHNIQUE TIP

Here are key points on going downhill with poles:

- Keep basic Nordic walking technique.
- Poles stay behind.
- Shorten stride.
- Use a higher frequency of steps (match arms).
- Bend knees.
- Land on the heel and roll onto foot.
- Get support from the poles.

Now here's the purpose of the poles when going downhill: As mentioned, you maintain the same basic Nordic walking technique. Well, almost. You still keep the poles at an angle; you still keep the opposite-arm, opposite-leg rhythm; and you still plant the poles. The difference going downhill is that you also apply some support on the poles as you plant them. This further decreases the impact on the joints. The steeper the hill, the less range of motion of the upper arm and the more support on the poles. If without the poles you have pain while going downhill, then you will be pleasantly surprised when using the poles. If you still feel pain, put more support on the poles, take even shorter strides, and walk slowly. In other words, let the poles take more weight off your joints. This is the main purpose of the poles as you descend. The first couple of times going downhill may feel awkward. As with anything else, practice makes master.

Nordic Walking Uphill

When you come down the hill, continue Nordic walking around on a flat surface. The first couple of times downhill may confuse your rhythm, so walking on a flat surface afterward will give you a chance to get back into it. As everything feels back to normal and you feel you have a good pace, start *counting* the rhythm on that flat surface. Every time you take a step with the right foot, say, "One," and every time you take a step with the left foot say, "Two."

When you have a solid one-two rhythm, approach the hill again, this time reversed: walking uphill. As you go up the hill, keep the one-two rhythm. It will push you to keep the same pace uphill as on the flat surface. In turn, the arms and legs have to work more aggressively when you're Nordic walking uphill. If you feel you are slipping with the poles, make sure you are planting the pole in the handshake position. Walking uphill, you probably have a natural

TECHNIQUE TIP

Here are key points on going uphill with poles:

- Maintain the basic Nordic walking technique.
- Count the one-two rhythm on a flat surface.
- Keep the same one-two rhythm and pace uphill, which requires more work from the arms and legs.
- Feel the natural leaning forward as one unit.

way of leaning forward (see figure 6.7). Make sure the forward lean is a straight line from the ankles to the head. This also means that you look slightly down, but absolutely not directly down. Some people have a tendency to take long and lazy strides as they try to increase the speed. If this sounds familiar, try to practice a leg stride that is shorter and more powerful. Now uphill the push from the ball of the foot comes in handy and activates those buttocks muscles. (Remember the basics of regular walking in the beginning of this chapter.) Try it: Correct handshake position, leaning forward as one unit, powerful arm and leg movement, and engaging the buttocks muscles via the push-off will make it easier to keep that one-two rhythm all the way up the hill.

Figure 6.7 Nordic walking uphill increases the heart rate by up to 30 beats per minute.

Conclusion

This chapter provides the tools to the basics in Nordic walking. Once you have built a solid Nordic walking foundation, you can add more fun. You can add the technique intensifiers in chapters 8 and 9. You can add Nordic winter walking and snowshoeing to your winter adventures. And you can add better walking habits. On the contrary, without the basics, it will be hard to progress. Compare it to building a house: If you don't have a solid foundation, it will not make sense to add more building materials to finish the house. So take the 5 to 15 minutes to learn basic Nordic walking. Then practice until you have mastered it before you add anything else. Those minutes will be the quickest educational investment that you have ever made with the most fruitful return on your well-being.

Summary of the Nordic Walking Techniques

Basic Nordic Walking (Level 1) (chapter 6)

- ☐ Find the natural walking rhythm: arm meets opposite leg.
- ☐ Plant pole with a firm squeeze in a handshake position.
- ☐ Push hand back to the hip and soften grip on the pole.

Urban Nordic Walking (Level 2) (chapter 8)

- ☐ Increase speed through footwork and legwork.
- ☐ Lean forward as one straight line from ankle to head.
- ☐ Softly rotate the upper body (rib cage), matching the lower-body (hip) rotation.

Nordic Trail Walking (Level 3) (chapter 9)

- ☐ Push hand past the hip and straighten the elbow.
- ☐ Open hand actively at the very end, keeping the fingers together and leading with the pinky finger.

CHAPTER 7

Components of a Nordic Walking Workout

> Be the change
> you want to see
> in the world.
>
> *Mahatma Gandhi*

By now you have probably realized that Nordic walking is a great way to improve your aerobic capacity—just like any other endurance sport. Whether you go Nordic walking just for fun or with a specific goal in mind, you need variation in the training. Doing the same exercise routine day in and day out is better than not doing anything at all, of course. But you can get even better results from doing a variety of activities as well as performing them differently from time to time. If you are a competitive athlete, you obviously need to follow a specific plan. On the other hand, if you are a fitness enthusiast who just wants to stay in shape, why not spice it up from time to time? People have a tendency to stay with things that are familiar. In this chapter you will find some easy ways to vary your Nordic walking workout to have more fun while getting into shape.

This chapter offers start-to-finish guidelines for a Nordic walking workout. Except for the trigger release, you will use the poles during each segment. Some of the components were covered in earlier chapters or will be covered more specifically in later chapters. Your work actually begins at home, where you will pack the fluid and food for the exercise. Before taking your first step of Nordic walking, start with a warm-up, which has three elements: trigger release, dynamic stretching, and a walking warm-up. Once the actual workout starts, you have several options. You can keep the same pace, vary the pace, vary the terrain, vary the surfaces, or vary the technique. If you wear a heart rate monitor, you can easily keep track of the changes in intensity as you vary the workout. Toward the end of the actual workout, you'll gradually slow down the pace and finish with some static stretches. Afterward it is always a good idea to refuel so that you can recover for the next Nordic walking workout.

SAFETY TIP

As with any exercise, there are risks, including increased heart stress and musculoskeletal injuries. A physician's examination is recommended for all participants who have any exercise restrictions and all participants over 40 years of age.

Check Fuel and Fluid

Before leaving home, make sure you bring enough water. As mentioned in chapter 5, food and water consumption during your Nordic walk depends on your individual needs, the intensity and duration of the Nordic walk, and the weather conditions. Following is a checklist for fluid and fuel before, during, and after exercise. For more details, review chapter 5.

Checklist for Fluid and Fuel Before, During, and After Exercise

Prepare Before Exercise

☐ A physically active person's daily total caloric intake should consist of 60 to 65 percent carbohydrate.

☐ Drink 16 ounces (about half a liter) of fluid 2 hours before exercise.

Replace During Exercise

☐ Drink 6 to 12 ounces (180-360 ml) of slightly chilled water every 15 to 20 minutes during exercise.

☐ Have enough water for exercise lasting less than 60 minutes.

☐ Add electrolyte replacement for exercise lasting more than 60 minutes.

☐ For a vigorous workout lasting more than 1 hour nonstop, add some easily absorbed carbohydrate, like glucose (for more details see page 103).

☐ Athletes who exercise nonstop for more than 3 hours should be aware of a medical condition called hyponatremia. (See page 103.)

Replenish After Exercise

☐ Drink 16 ounces (half a liter) of fluid for every pound (half a kilogram) lost.

☐ Within 2 hours of the workout, replenish the glycogen stores. Combine carbohydrate and protein: 4 grams of carbohydrate for every 1 gram of protein.

TECHNIQUE TIP
Good Posture and Form

- Keep the abdomen lightly pulled in.
- Keep the shoulders gently back and down.
- Keep the body aligned.

Warm-Up Phase

Why can't you just start sprinting and forget the warm-up? Think about this for a moment. Do you enjoy waking up to a loud, irritating buzz that scares you out of bed, or do you enjoy waking up to a soothing sound that gradually increases in volume until you are ready to glide out of bed? I hope you picked the second option, which is why it *feels* better to gradually prepare the body for exercise. What better way of getting a self-massage? That is mainly what trigger release is all about—finding the knots and kneading them until they give in a little bit. You can do this any time of day, but the best time is before the dynamic warm-up. You can do it in the convenience of your home. Go back to page 24 in chapter 2 and follow the instructions. All you need is a foam roller and some patience. The slight discomfort you feel at first as you find a trigger point should diminish after 30 seconds. The releasing result makes it all worth it. If you have some stubborn knots, you will feel them slowly disappear in discomfort after consistent trigger release for at least two weeks. Patience and persistence pay off.

As mentioned in chapter 2, it is always a good idea to increase the body temperature, get the blood circulating, loosen the muscles, and improve the joint function to prepare the body for the physical activity. You can do this through dynamic stretching, which involves body movements that will take the joints through the full range of motion. You will start with a small range of motion and then increase to a comfortable range of motion. It is a gentle awakening of the muscles and joints.

TECHNIQUE TIP

- Trigger release eases tension in the muscles.
- Dynamic stretches warm up the muscles and joints to prepare the body for the specific activity to be performed.

Dynamic Stretches

Follow these instructions for each of the stretches that follow:

- Practice good form (review the three reminders at the beginning of this chapter).
- Gently move the joint in a comfortable range of motion.
- Increase the range of motion if the body agrees.
- Move in a controlled manner.
- Repeat each movement 10 times on each joint.

SWING AND BOUNCE (LEGS, ARMS, AND SHOULDERS)

Hold on to the poles in the middles, swing the arms gently back and forth *(a)*, and gradually introduce bouncing in the knees to match the rhythm of the arm movement *(b)*.

TOE RAISES (ANKLES)

Place the poles vertically in front of you *(a)*. Exhale and raise the heels as high off the ground as possible *(b)*. Pause at the top. Inhale and lower the heels slowly.

SAFETY TIP

Keep the asphalt paws on during the Nordic warm-up and whenever you have the poles in a horizontal position above the ground. Even with the paws on during your Nordic warm-up, keep a slightly longer than pole-length space between you and the people next to you.

WALKING LUNGE (HIPS AND KNEES)

Start with feet parallel *(a)*. Place the poles in front of you farther than normal. Reach forward with the paws (or spike tips) of the pole. Take a long step forward *(b)*, landing on the heel, rolling onto the foot, and gently kneeling down with both legs into a lunge position to a comfortable range of motion. Push away with the ball of the foot of the back leg *(c)* and without putting down the foot, take another long step *(d)*. Get some additional help from the poles to get back up or to maintain balance. Repeat the movements using alternate legs until you have "walked" a total of 20 steps.

CHEST OPENER

Place the poles in front of you *(a)*. Lean slightly forward, using very little support from the poles but more from your abdomen. Return to upright, making a big circle with the arms to stretch the chest *(b)*. Increase the chest stretch by squeezing the shoulder blades gently.

a   b

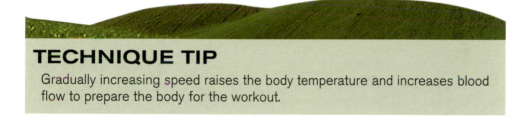

TECHNIQUE TIP

Gradually increasing speed raises the body temperature and increases blood flow to prepare the body for the workout.

Maybe so far you have done all the warm-up indoors and it's time to step outdoors. Or maybe you just finished the dynamic stretching outdoors and you can't wait to get going. In both scenarios, start Nordic walking from a slow to a comfortable speed. Give it a good 5 to 10 minutes or until you feel warm. The body needs time to prepare for the higher demands of the coming workout phase. The blood needs to come up to speed to provide enough oxygen and nutrients to the working muscles. Otherwise the muscles will not be able to perform optimally and you will run out of energy before you know it.

Workout Phase

As mentioned in chapter 2, there are many benefits of endurance training, but this chapter mainly focuses on the cardiorespiratory benefits. The other benefits will be regarded as a nice bonus. The ways of increasing endurance are based on recommendations from the American College of Sports Medicine (ACSM). There are four factors to take into account. First the *activity* you perform needs to be rhythmic and involve large muscle groups, and it must be performed uninterrupted over an extended period. Walking is a great example. Anoth... ...er is *duration*. You need to stay in the workout phase 20 to 60 minutes... that those minutes do not include the time you spend warming ... ing down. How often—*frequency*—is also important. The recom...

ENDURANCE TRAINING FACTORS

Factors to take into account to improve aerobic capacity.

- Activity
- Duration
- Frequency
- Intensity

three to five times a week, but it also depends on the intensity. If you work at a high intensity, then three days a week should be enough. But if the intensity is lower, five days a week may be needed. *Intensity* is the last factor but one of the most important. The American College of Sports Medicine (2006) recommends a wide range of intensity from 64 to 94 percent of your maximum heart rate (HRmax) to improve your aerobic functioning. That means that a deconditioned person may reach aerobic benefits from working out five times a week at a low intensity of 64 to 70 percent of HRmax. However, a person who is already aerobically active would benefit from working out only three times a week but at a higher intensity from 77 to 94 percent of HRmax.

It is easy to keep track of intensity with a heart rate monitor. Without one you need to keep track of it by checking your pulse manually, which requires you to stop to check it. The second you stop, your heart rate goes down, so make sure you take it for the first 6 seconds. Multiply that number by 10 and you have the heartbeats per minute.

How do you know what number to keep track of? You have to do some calculation to estimate your maximum heart rate, which is based on your age. Use the formula of 220 minus your age. If you are 30 years old, your maximum heart rate is 190. It is only an estimate that does not take your fitness status into consideration. You can be 30 years old and in good shape or in bad shape, but this formula will give you the same result: 190. That is why it is only an estimate. There are other ways to figure out or at least get closer to your individual maximum heart rate or the recommended range of intensity. The easiest one is to use a heart rate monitor that has a feature called *own zone*.

TECHNIQUE TIP
Use endurance training options to add variety to training and intensity.

Various ways of training (continuous, interval, hill) were covered in chapter 2. Following is a list of additional ways to vary training and intensity.

Options in Designing Endurance Workouts

- **Continuous** is same speed and same intensity.
- **Interval** is varying speed and intensity in one- to five-minute bouts.
- **Surfaces** are the types of land. Asphalt may be the easiest surface; grass and dirt may be more difficult. Sand, especially soft sand, provides a moderate- to high-intensity workout.
- **Terrain** can be flat or hilly. Flat terrain is easy; hills, especially steep ones, provide an excellent way to intensify the workout.
- **Techniques** are the methods used. The basic Nordic walking technique is easy to learn. The technique intensifiers in chapter 8 are more difficult, and the intensifiers in chapter 9 can be quite challenging.

TECHNIQUE TIP
Estimate Your Heart Rate Zone

Use the example of a 30-year-old person (bpm = beats per minute).

- Maximum heart rate is $220 - 30$ (age) $= 190$ bpm.
- Recommended range is 64 to 70 percent (lower limit) and 77 to 94 percent (higher limit) of maximum heart rate.
- Lower limits are as follows:
  - $.64 \times 190 = 122$ bpm
  - $.70 \times 190 = 133$ bpm
- Higher limit is $.94 \times 190 = 179$ bpm.

Conclusion: Mr. A and Mr. B are both 30 years old, but Mr. A is just starting out with an aerobic exercise program, whereas Mr. B is used to aerobic activities on a regular basis. For Mr. A to improve his aerobic capacity, he needs to keep the heart rate (pulse) between 121 and 133. This is the estimated heart rate zone for Mr. A and he also needs to consider working out five times a week for 30 minutes or more each time (excluding warm-up and cool-down). For Mr. B to improve his aerobic capacity, he needs to keep the heart rate (pulse) between 133 and 179. This is the estimated heart rate zone for Mr. B and he will be fine with working out three times a week for 20 to 30 minutes each time (excluding warm-up and cool-down).

Cool-Down Phase

You are getting close to home and you can't wait to go inside to stretch. Slow down the pace gradually for five minutes before you come to a complete stop. Cooling down gradually is just as important as warming up. During the workout, the pace is pretty fast: Blood circulation, heart rate, and blood pressure have increased to meet the demand of the intensity of the workout. If you abruptly stop, you do not give these systems a fair warning to finish what they started. The blood still has several jobs to conclude; one is to remove waste products. If the blood flow deceases abruptly, the removal of waste slows down. Another task involves delivering enough oxygen to areas that still have a high demand. Failure to do so can cause dizziness as well as more serious cardiovascular complications. Be safe—progressively push on the brakes for five minutes.

Unless you want to feel stiff the following day, make sure you take a few minutes to stretch the muscles that you have just worked. Any muscle work will shorten them. Your job is to ensure they get back to normal length. It is like resetting the muscles for the next workout. In addition, these stretches feel so good; if they don't, you're not doing them correctly. Apply the following instructions, especially the part about mild discomfort. People think that if it doesn't hurt, it is not accomplishing anything. This "no pain, no gain" philosophy is old school. Static stretching at the end of the workout should be regarded as the reward. Enjoy it to the fullest and integrate a moment of appreciation of the workout you just completed. Focus on the breathing and further relax the mind before getting back to your busy day.

Static Stretches

Follow these instructions for each of the stretches that follow:

- Practice good form (review the three reminders at the beginning of this chapter).
- Get into a correct position (check the photos).
- Stretch the muscle until you feel a mild discomfort (tension).
- On every exhalation (outward breath), feel tension decrease in the muscle.
- Hold the position for 20 to 30 seconds.
- Gently ease out of the stretch.

TECHNIQUE TIP

Begin the cool-down phase by gradually decreasing speed to prepare the body to return to the normal resting state. End the workout with static stretches to lengthen the muscles to their original length or farther if needed.

CALF STRETCH

Place both poles in front of you with some space in between the poles *(a)*. Lean both poles away from you and place the heel of one foot at the base of the poles. The whole foot should be leaning on the poles. As you straighten the body, pull both poles toward you *(b)*. Stop the pulling when you feel a mild discomfort in the calf.

BACK STRETCH

Place both poles shoulder-width apart half your body length in front of you *(a)*. Slightly bend your knees, straighten your arms, and keep the ears in line with the arms. In a perfect world, the back would be parallel to the ground, but your back or hamstring muscles may not allow this. Stop in a position where you feel mild discomfort on the side from the lower back to the armpit. You may also have some discomfort in the hamstrings. After 30 seconds, pull in the abdomen and gently return by curling up slowly *(b)*.
It should feel like a wave starting in the abdomen and ending with the head curling up *(c)*.

BUTTOCK STRETCH

Place both poles in front of you. Swing one foot up on top of the opposite knee. Sit down on one leg. (Good thing you have the support from the poles.) Make sure you lead the sitting by dipping the buttocks. Avoid moving the knee past the toes. There is a slight forward lean of the back. If you are able to sit down 90 degrees (with your knee behind the toes) and you want to increase the stretch in the hip and buttocks area, you can lean the back forward more.

QUAD STRETCH

After the last stretch, the front thighs get tired, so it's a perfect time to stretch them. Build an upside-down V with the poles to create more support from the poles. Place one hand on top of both grips of the poles. Take the other hand and gently bring the foot toward the buttocks. Feel the mild discomfort in the quadriceps muscle (front of the thigh).

Here are some common mistakes in this stretch: The knee points outward *(correct form is to point the knee downward)*, the lower back arches too much *(correct form is to tilt the pelvis slightly under to a neutral position and pull the abdomen in slightly to lock the pelvic position)*, and the whole body tilts *(correct form is a tall posture)*. If you struggle with this stretch, you have other options: Do another quad stretch, hold on to something sturdier, or switch to the next stretch—hip flexor—because you may find that you feel that stretch somewhat in the quads as well.

HIP FLEXOR STRETCH

Kneel down on one knee. Make sure the hip is lined up with the knee that touches the ground. You should be able to draw a straight line between the two joints. Make sure the other knee is lined up with the ankle that touches the ground in front of you. The back should be straight—no leaning forward or backward. Feel the stretch or more like a slight pull at the top of the front thigh. If you want to increase the stretch, tuck the pelvis in and under and tighten the buttock of the leg that is being stretched.

CHEST STRETCH

Place the poles wide apart in front of you *(a)*. With good form, squeeze the shoulder blades together and then let the poles fall farther apart *(b)*. Feel the mild discomfort in the upper chest. Check your core. Very often people arch the lower back to assist in the chest stretch. This is counterproductive. Maintain the stability of the lower back by keeping the core activated.

TRICEPS STRETCH

Grab the grip of only one pole and bring the whole pole behind you *(a)*. The top of the pole is facing up and the bottom of the pole is facing down. Straighten the arm fully toward the sky (or ceiling if you are indoors). The hand that is free grabs the bottom of the pole and starts pulling it down toward the ground. In order for this to happen, you have to allow the straight arm to bend *(b)*. Keep pulling the pole down by shifting grips higher and higher up on the pole. Stop when you feel a mild discomfort in the back of the arm that started out straight. Go only as far down as the range of motion allows. Check your core. As always, maintain the stability of the lower back by keeping the core activated.

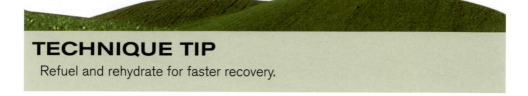

TECHNIQUE TIP

Refuel and rehydrate for faster recovery.

After the workout, you have a two-hour window in which to fill up the glycogen storage in your body. The best way is to eat a combination of carbohydrate and protein. As mentioned in chapter 5, mix 4 grams of carbohydrate for every 1 gram of protein. Regarding the fluid in your body, estimate the loss by getting on a scale before and after a workout. For every pound (half a kilogram) lost, drink 16 ounces (half a liter) of fluid.

Conclusion

Have you ever noticed the difference in the bodies of various athletes? A sprinter is solid and powerful. A marathon runner is lean and has lots of endurance. What they have in common is a training plan. However, their workouts differ because they are based on the sport each athlete performs. If you want to reach a specific goal, you have to train for it and also know *how* to train for it. This chapter provides you with a start-to-finish structure of a Nordic walking workout. You now know how to warm up, how to vary the workout, and how to stretch at the end. If you are a novice, it will be a good idea for you to follow the format until it becomes automatic. After this chapter, you will be able to include all the right elements when you design your own aerobic workout. Remember to vary the training sessions to avoid boredom. It's all about having fun and moving forward: Make a change, reach a goal.

NORDIC WALKER TIP

For your FREE one-week Nordic walking workout calendar visit www. NordicBody.com.

Structure of a Nordic Walking Workout

1. Check fuel and fluids
2. Warm-up phase:
   - Trigger release
   - Dynamic warm-up with poles
   - Gradual increase of speed for 5 to 10 minutes
3. Workout phase:
   - Factors
     - Time: 20 to 60 minutes
     - Intensity: 64 to 70 percent (lower limit) and 77 to 94 percent (higher limit) of your maximum heart rate
   - Options
     - Continuous
     - Intervals
     - Surfaces
     - Terrain
     - Techniques
4. Cool-down phase:
   - Gradual decrease of speed for 5 minutes
   - Static stretches
   - Refueling and rehydration

Applying the estimated time and intensity factors to your Nordic walking workout three to five days a week will improve your aerobic capacity.

CHAPTER 8

Urban Nordic Walking

Everything is given at the price of an effort.

Leonardo da Vinci

Honestly, the first time you saw a pair of Nordic walking poles, did you think right away about using them in the city on the sidewalks? Maybe you did. Most people find it peculiar to see people Nordic walking in the city. Once they try it, though, they change their minds. The reason people look at you so curiously is that they don't know what you are doing. You are a pioneer. Enlighten them. Tell them it's called Nordic walking and that it burns more calories than regular walking. Who cares if people stare and ask strange questions like "Where is the snow?", if you can gain more benefits than you would with regular walking? Remember that you burn 20 to 46 percent more calories, strengthen the upper body, and put less stress on your joints than regular walking. Did you know that you may be part of writing Nordic walking history? Maybe you are the very first person in your town to Nordic walk. Somebody has to be first, and then others will follow. It's like fashion: Did you stare at the first person you saw who wore bell-bottom pants? You can't help but stare at anything you have not seen before. Would you stare at a purple dog walking down the street? Of course, because it's natural. If you still do feel a little self-conscious, you may want to team up with a buddy and hit the streets together the first couple of times. Once you do it, the great feeling and benefits of Nordic walking will override the awkward feeling of self-consciousness. Eventually you will start thinking, *Why isn't everybody Nordic walking?* Don't they know what they are missing? Probably not. So you have to be the one telling them or, better yet, let them try it out. It's the best feeling to see and hear people's positive reactions the first time they try Nordic walking.

One of the best things about Nordic walking is that you can start right outside your door in the middle of the city. No more driving to exercise. For somebody who is in fairly good shape, basic Nordic walking may not be enough. Don't worry; there are ways to take it up a notch. Try changing surfaces: Go from asphalt to grass to sand. Then test different paces. Changing speed not only makes it more fun but also changes the intensity. Find a hilly part of the city and you will soon be huffing and puffing. Finally, you can increase the intensity by adding more walking techniques. You can stay within the city limits and get a great workout. Just make sure you are as cautious as a regular pedestrian. Listening to your favorite music while working out is very inspirational and cuts you off from the outside. Although this can be de-stressing and enjoyable, you need to be alert enough to know what's happening around you, especially while crossing the streets. Hit the streets safely!

Explore the City With Nordic Walking

The ideal way to introduce Nordic walking is of course in a beautiful outdoor environment where you have access to all kinds of surfaces and terrain. I have traveled all over the world to teach Nordic walking to both fitness professionals and the public. While some destinations have not been the best suited for teaching Nordic walking, somehow it has always been made possible. You can try Nordic walking indoors in a long hallway; you can try it in an alley or even in a parking lot. You can Nordic walk on a busy street that eventually takes you to a peaceful green park in the middle of the city. You name it, and any place is possible for Nordic walking. However, there is one element that always needs to be present to make an introduction to Nordic walking complete: a hill. If you're in fairly good shape, you can intensify a workout with even a slight incline. An even steeper hill will really get the heart pumping. It's all about exploring your city to find those treasures.

The best way to see a new city is through the eyes of the people who reside there. See chapter 4 for specific routes created by local people. The second best way to discover a new city is on foot. Yes, you can cover more areas by car. Even on a bike, a skateboard, and in-line skates you can see more in one day than by walking. But by foot you notice more. You can easily stop, look at a map, and be more spontaneous as you create a Nordic walking city adventure. You will encounter the most charming places tucked away or hidden like a secret, places that *only you* can find by walking.

You may not even know your own city that well. And, sadly enough, some areas of your city may not be that walking friendly. It is my hope and mission that this will change more rapidly. Imagine if all cities were walking friendly. Then people would walk more and thus get enough physical activity to maintain their health or become healthier. Explore your city while Nordic walking. Locate that charming street that feels like a community. Find a grassy park where you

I travel not to go anywhere, but to go.

Robert L. Stevenson

can take the paws off the poles to go Nordic walking. Maybe you live close to a beach, where the soft sand will provide one of the toughest workouts you may have ever experienced.

Surfaces and Locations

Depending on where you live, you either will have lots of options in regard to surfaces or just a few. Try them all out and see how different the poles feel on different surfaces. Following are some reminders on handling the poles safely on several surfaces within city limits.

SAFETY TIP

Nordic Walking on City Sidewalks

Surface: Asphalt
Location: City sidewalks

- Keep the asphalt paws on.
- Nordic walk in single file on sidewalks.
- Give space to other people passing by.
- Cautiously cross the streets: Temporarily stop distractions such as listening to music, talking on the cell phone, or talking to a walking buddy.
- Safely wave the poles to make sure drivers see you as you cross a street.

Nordic Walking in City Parks

Surface: Grass
Location: City parks

- Safely remove the asphalt paws (spike tips exposed). (See page 109 in chapter 5)
- When not Nordic walking and when spike tips are exposed, carry the poles vertically.
- Keep a distance from people behind you, to your side, and in front of you.

Nordic Walking on City Beaches or Deserts

Surface: Sand
Location: City beach or desert

- A strong core is required for Nordic sand walking.
- If you're a first-time Nordic sand walker, keep the paws on.
- If you're a seasoned Nordic sand walker, safely remove the paw.
- Avoid wearing sandals.

Urban Nordic Walking Workout and Intensifiers

Urban Nordic walking builds on the foundation of basic Nordic walking (see chapter 6) and takes Nordic walking to another level for those who wish to make the workout more difficult. It is the perfect form of exercise for the typical city person: easily accessible, productive, and efficient. You'll produce better results at work if you take a break. Go Nordic walking to decompress, to think clearly, and to get away from being indoors all day. Return rejuvenated and recharged to handle another fast-paced and productive work day. Make sure you look at the time you start because time flies when you go Nordic walking. Suggested duration is 30 to 60 minutes and the intensity should be within the range of 77 to 94 percent of your maximum heart rate. This intensity is based on you being aerobically active on a regular basis. Choose a lower limit when going for a longer duration than 30 minutes and chose a higher to go for 20 to 30 minutes. (See page 141 in chapter 7 if you need a reminder on calculating this.) For most of us, 94 percent of maximum heart rate will take us into an anaerobic stage and thus we would only be able to be there for a brief time. The best way to find out your individual heart rate zone is to schedule a sub-maximal walking test with a health and fitness professional.

After perfecting the basic Nordic walking technique, you are ready to take the workout to another level. There are many ways of intensifying and varying the training. Some are easier, and others are more difficult. Following are some ideas. Try them and find what works best for you. The specific examples make it easier to integrate them into your Nordic walking workout. The descriptions of intervals and hills were covered in chapter 2. And the focus for all the intensifiers is during the dry season.

Changing Intensity With Surfaces

Some people think it is easier to Nordic walk on asphalt or cement. Some people think grass is easier. Try both and see what you think. With grass you can't cheat—you are forced to get good traction as you plant the poles. The exposed spike tip digs into the grass. With asphalt you can get away with just tapping the pole as you plant. Unfortunately this diminishes the engagement of the upper-body muscles. For many people, grass will feel choppy the first couple of times. For the most part it is about getting accustomed to a new surface. If it continues to feel choppy, try refining the handshake position. Basically focus

TECHNIQUE TIP

Vary intensity by changing surfaces: asphalt, grass, and sand.

on bringing the elbow in front of the body. Instead of gluing the elbow to the waist, free the elbow—both when you plant and when you push back. It is very common for only one arm—usually the left one for someone whose right side is dominant—to feel choppy. For a right-dominant person, over the years the muscles of the right arm have developed a better relationship with the nerves that control the muscles. Unless you have any nerve damage, the left arm can catch up. Try to let the left arm imitate the movement of the right arm. A frequent incident on asphalt is that you feel that you are slipping. Again, refine the handshake position but also check the status of your paws. They may be worn out and as a result you won't get good traction.

Although the opinions differ about Nordic walking on asphalt and grass, everyone will agree that sand is an excellent intensifier. The first time you Nordic walk on sand, keep the paws on to avoid sinking down too much. Sure, you sink down with the shoes as well, but shoes cover a larger area and therefore you sink less with the feet than with the pointed spike tip on the pole. Picture your poles sinking down more than the feet. The poles shorten, which forces you to lean forward more. The farther forward you lean, the more taxing it is on the lower-back muscles unless you have a strong core that is made for

A fun and healthy Nordic walking adventure in the city.

endurance, meaning that you are able to keep the core activated even after 30 minutes of Nordic walking, especially in the sand. You can build core strength (see chapter 2). Unless you have a strong core to protect the lower back, keep the paws on, or maybe even reconsider whether you should Nordic walk on sand just yet. The softer the sand, the more difficult the workout. You might try walking closer to the water so that you're on more compact sand. Just be observant about the uneven terrain closer to the water. You don't want to walk too long in a tilted body position.

Changing Intensity With Intervals

For competitive athletes, there are certain criteria for the structure of aerobic interval training based on their goals. For everyone else, the great thing about intervals is that anyone at any fitness level can do it, and the only rule is to change the speed. You decide how fast or slow you want to walk, and you decide how long you want the intervals to last. You also get to decide how many intervals you want to do. Aside from the advantage of making a Nordic walking workout more fun, intervals help you reach another intensity level. However briefly you stay at a high intensity level, the heart will get a taste of what you are demanding. Next time, the heart will be better prepared for the demand and eventually even expect it. After some training, that intensity level may not even feel like much of a challenge to you and you can stay there for a longer time.

Test various paces and play with some of the following examples. Decide what slow, moderate, and high intensity mean to you. The slow walk should be easy, the moderate walk should be somewhat difficult, and the high intensity should be the fastest speed you have in store. A heart rate monitor is the perfect tool to help you add an objective point of view. After you estimate your maximum heart rate based on your age (220 minus your age), then figure out 64, 70, and 94 percent of your estimated heart rate. Use those as guidelines for the easy, moderate, and intense paces. For a 30-year-old, an easy pace is 122 beats per minute (bpm), 133 bpm is moderate, and 179 bpm is high intensity. Remember, these are just estimated guidelines. Maybe the 133 pulse is too easy for you when you try to keep a moderate pace. Use your own subjective feeling and either increase or decrease the intensity so it feels somewhat difficult during the moderate pace stage. One caution about speed and Nordic walking is that it is easy to forget about the technique. Some of the fastest walkers have a bad habit of hardly using the poles. Initially if your walk is slow, you will most likely feel how you increase the speed with the help of

TECHNIQUE TIP

Vary intensity with intervals: Change speed every one to five minutes.

the poles. However, if you already are a fast walker, pay attention to using the poles more. Your fastest walk then is not with poles; it is without poles. The poles provide all the benefits mentioned in chapter 1, and those benefits are based on correct use of the poles.

As you try the various ways of doing intervals, know that you can choose to do only one part of the workout using intervals. If you want the workout phase to be 40 minutes, you can do continuous training (keeping the same speed and intensity) for 10 minutes, then do interval training for 20 minutes, and then finish as you started with 10 minutes of continuous training. The workout phase does not include the time you spend warming up and cooling down.

If it's difficult to keep track of the time, then use various landmarks instead: "I will walk fast for one block and then walk slowly for half a block." "I will walk fast until I reach the stairs and then I will walk slowly until I reach the post office."

EXAMPLES OF INTERVALS DURING THE WORKOUT PHASE

- 5 minutes at a moderate intensity, 2 minutes at an easy intensity, and repeat the cycle 3 times = 21 minutes in the workout phase
- 1 minute at a high intensity, 1 minute at an easy intensity, and repeat the cycle 10 times = 20 minutes in the workout phase
- 2 minutes at a moderate to high intensity, 1 minute at an easy intensity, and repeat the cycle 7 times = 21 minutes in the workout phase

Changing Intensity With Hills

As mentioned in chapter 2, hill training is an excellent way to increase your aerobic capacity. Chapter 6 covers the up-and-down hill technique for Nordic walking. Start with smaller and shorter hills and then progress to steeper and longer hills. Going up is easy; just keep the same rhythm as you do when Nordic walking on flat terrain. This will automatically force the arms and legs to work more aggressively. The uphill part will increase the intensity. You will need to practice and perfect the downhill technique in order to avoid injuries; review the technique in chapter 6. Following are a few examples of integrating hill training into your Nordic walking workout to increase the intensity as well as keeping track of your progress.

TECHNIQUE TIP

Vary intensity by changing terrain, such as hills.

EXAMPLES OF HILL TRAINING DURING THE WORKOUT PHASE

• Build your Nordic walking workout around hills in your neighborhood. One example is to go up one hill for one block on the left side and down on the right side. Then continue to the parallel street and climb that hill the same way. If you have a stretch of parallel streets with hills, you can keep going for a long time and return the same way, like a sideways serpentine.

• Choose a hill that is challenging. You may not be able to reach the top the first time. Check your watch at the bottom of the hill and check it again at the top or the point you are able to climb to. How long did it take you? Write down the time in a calendar and include the landmark, unless you reached the top. Also note how you felt at the top (or landmark) by using a scale of 1 to 10 (10 indicates that it was so exhausting that you could not have taken another step). Retime yourself in a month. If you have included hills consistently (three times a week), you should notice some progress either in your time or in your subjective feeling of fatigue (the scale of 1 to 10).

• Use hill training as interval training. Find a hill that takes approximately a minute to climb. Use the uphill portion as the high-intensity part of the interval, and use the downhill portion as the resting part. Do as many as you can—even one cycle will work. Another time, up it to two cycles, and so on.

Use a heart rate monitor to check your pulse while going uphill; otherwise you may not believe the amount of increased intensity compared to Nordic walking on flat terrain. The rating of perceived exertion stays the same whether or not you use poles while going uphill. The intensity, however, can increase as much as 30 heartbeats per minute while you're going uphill with poles!

Changing Intensity With Walking Techniques

Now it's time to increase the intensity by using your body as the main tool. Remember that Nordic walking is an enhancement of regular walking. This is the reason you are encouraged to review the basics of regular walking technique in chapter 6. Some things you do naturally and some things you have to put some effort into. Following are three examples (foot/legwork, lean forward, rib cage

TECHNIQUE TIP

Vary the intensity by applying additional walking techniques: foot/legwork, lean forward, and rib cage rotation.

rotation) of what you can integrate into your Nordic walking workout, assuming you have nearly perfected basic Nordic walking. Otherwise the examples may only become distractions instead of useful tools for taking the workout up a notch. Use one example at a time. Let the body get accustomed to the new instructions for a few Nordic walking workouts. When it feels natural and automatic, meaning you don't have to think, then you are ready to apply the next example.

Use Footwork and Legwork to Increase Speed

To avoid confusion during this process, focus on the same foot and leg. Then isolate the opposite foot and leg when repeating the process. When you feel both sides are working well, integrate them. If it's still too much, you can always go back to isolating until it feels natural and automatic. The footwork will encompass the first five steps in the basics of regular walking. If necessary, review the details in chapter 6. If you feel confident, add it to the basic Nordic walking technique.

Start with being aware of how you land with the center of the heel (see figure 8.1). Continue to roll onto the rest of the foot. The landing and rolling should be close to soundless. As you roll onto the ball of the foot (base of the toes), the heel comes off the ground. Push the ball of the foot down and back into the ground. At the same time you push off with the ball of the foot, you activate the very bottom of the buttock (see figure 8.2). This push-off action propels the body forward. Walk around and feel how you push off with the base of the toes (specifically between the first and second toes), activating the buttock of the same leg. This push-off action increases the speed and is useful during intervals.

Figure 8.1 Land with the heel.

Figure 8.2 Push off with the ball of the foot and buttock to increase speed.

Lean Forward From Heel to Head to Increase Speed

As you go uphill, you instinctively lean forward. From the side, it should look as though you lean as one unit from heel to head (see figure 8.3). Do not bend in the middle or in the upper back. This position requires good core activation. As you practice Nordic walking uphill, feel and be aware of the inclination to lean forward. Continue this leaning sensation on *flat terrain* right after the hill. It should feel like you are falling forward. Note the increase in speed.

Rotate Lower Rib Cage to Engage More Muscles

Remember practicing the slight rotation around the solar plexus in chapter 6? Well, it is time to apply it to your Nordic walking technique. If your back is stiff, this will be a nice add-on to stretch and move those muscles. Review the slight twist of the torso without the poles (see step 9, page 122, in chapter 6). Divide the body into two parts: upper and lower. Their meeting place is in the solar plexus. This is the axis of the rotation. Focus on initiating a slight rotation in the solar plexus (see figure 8.4). This soft upper-body rotation matches the lower-body rotation. The deep initiation of rotational movement results in the movement of the shoulders and the hips. It is very important that you keep the core activated and the shoulder blades stabilized during the slight rotation. Avoid crossing the arms in front of you. Make sure that the arms swing straight forward and back. While this internal rotational movement makes

Figure 8.3 Lean forward in a straight line to increase speed.

Figure 8.4 A slight rib cage rotation engages more muscles as well as relaxes them.

NORDIC WALKER TIP

Here are some other urban Nordic walking adventures:

- Spend the day at the beach or at a park with friends and family while some or all of you go Nordic walking. Afterward, meet for a healthful picnic.
- Go Nordic winter walking when the snow arrives.
- Try Nordic snowshoeing in the wintry park.

more muscles work, it also creates an efficient way for the body to maintain balance while walking. Keep this awareness whether you Nordic walk or go for a stroll without the poles. It improves your gait and releases tension in the back, chest, shoulders, and neck. That's a great bonus!

Conclusion

Whether you use basic Nordic walking or add the three walking techniques from this chapter, you can Nordic walk everywhere within the city limits. This chapter is mainly for people who want to put some more effort into a workout. By adding all the other intensifiers, you should be able to stay close to home yet get a satisfying workout. Enjoy yourself, and be safe!

Factors and Options in an Urban Nordic Walking Workout (Level 2)

Factors

- ☐ Time: 20 to 60 minutes (excluding the time for warm-up and cool-down)
- ☐ Intensity: 77 to 94 percent of your maximum heart rate

Options

- ☐ Continuous
- ☐ Surfaces: asphalt, grass, sand
- ☐ Intervals: 1- to 5-minute bouts
- ☐ Terrain: hills
- ☐ Walking techniques: add foot/legwork, lean forward, slight rib cage rotation

CHAPTER 9

Nordic Trail Walking

To climb steep hills requires a slow pace at first.

Shakespeare

Seeing somebody with poles on a mountain trail is very common. In that environment, you will not get the same strange looks as you would in the city. People who hike understand the concept right away. Maybe they use one or two poles for assistance up and down the hills, or they *wished* they had poles when they meet you. Trekking or hiking poles have been around long enough for people to know about or experience using them. It is a familiar sight and the benefits are obvious. Nordic walking on trails, also called Nordic hiking, is different from trekking—enough to make a difference in the benefits and purpose. Whereas trekking and hiking poles assist you while you go up and down hills by providing support and taking weight off the joints, Nordic walking and Nordic hiking exist to give you a great workout. You don't use the Nordic walking poles only to climb more easily or take the stress off the joints while descending; you keep using the poles on flat ground as well to keep the heart rate elevated. Simply put, Nordic walking is about wasting energy (burning calories), while trekking is about saving energy. And the techniques are different, as you will discover in this chapter.

The techniques you have explored so far in basic Nordic walking (Level 1) and urban Nordic walking (Level 2) are different from trekking mainly because of the planting of the pole. In Nordic walking your pole stays at an angle; in trekking you plant it vertically. Other distinctions are described in chapter 3, where various pole sports are compared based on their purpose. When you get into the mountains, there are natural intensifiers and challenges. The surface may be dirt in most parts, but most likely there will be loose gravel and rocks. The terrain is uneven and you have to watch your step as well as where you plant the poles. The steeper hills are a welcome challenge and sometimes the sole purpose to leave the city behind. Another purpose is to be close to nature sounds instead of city noise. Previous chapters provided examples of changing the speed and integrating city hills into your Nordic walking workout. The approach to speed and hills in this chapter is similar but with a few new surprise moves. If you feel you have the skills of basic and urban Nordic walking under control, add more use of the poles: Push past the hip and open the hand. It will advance your Nordic walking workout.

Explore Local Trails

When I moved to Los Angeles, I was pleasantly surprised by all the local hiking available. It's not exactly the first thing you equate with Los Angeles. Disneyland, Universal Studios, Hollywood, and Sunset Boulevard are more closely associated with the Los Angeles area. After a friend showed me the Santa Monica Mountains by motorcycle, I decided to find out more about the possibility of hiking in the area. A local outdoor equipment store had some current books on local hiking. Every Sunday became the day to explore a new trail from the book. Today I don't need a book or a map to find my way around—I have a menu of hikes to choose from. There is the hike if I have time to drive only 10 minutes. There is the hike for the out-of-town visitor whom I want to inspire with some beautiful waterfalls. There is the easy hike that anyone can do. There is the five-hour hike that people have to train for. There is the long hike with a perfect place halfway to rest, to snack, or to meditate. It is not recommended to go alone, but if you don't know anyone who is up for a hike, find out about hiking groups in your area. The Sierra Club is an organization with chapters across the United States that, among other things, provide members with information about various hikes locally, regionally, nationally, and even internationally. In chapter 4 of this book, you can find out about specific Nordic walking routes or hikes all over the world. In appendix B, you will find resources about Nordic walking activities, classes, events, and trips. Many hotels and spas offer Nordic walking or hiking packages. Maybe your next vacation will involve some Nordic hiking?

Surfaces and Location

Most trails in the mountains have dirt as the main surface. Try to choose well-maintained and marked trails to make it easier on your ankles. Following are some reminders on handling the poles as well as handling yourself safely on a local mountain trail.

Travelers, there is no path, paths are made by walking.

Antonio Machado

Nordic Trail Walking Workout and Intensifiers

Though there usually is some driving involved, a visit in nature is worth the time spent getting there. You will return with a healthier and happier body *and* mind. Please arrange for carpooling if you are going with a group. It gives you more time with friends and family and saves you money on fuel, and you contribute to preserving the environment. Think about protecting the environment as you are walking around in nature. Chapter 5 gives you some things to think about. Be respectful of both nature and wildlife. Even though this book focuses on marked trails that take no longer than three hours to traverse and avoids the unmarked trails, be aware of the fact that you are entering territory that belongs to the wildlife.

As always, check the time when you start. Time flies while Nordic walking, and you want to ensure you finish the workout before sunset. Otherwise it will be very difficult to see where you are stepping unless you have the luxury of not only a marked trail but also a lit trail.

Nordic trail walking (Level 3) builds on the various walking techniques you explored in urban Nordic walking (Level 2). If you are ready to add more techniques, this time focusing on the pole as well as the body, do it. It will advance your Nordic walking workout. Suggested duration is one to three hours, and the suggested intensity can be anywhere within the range of 77 to 94 percent of your maximum heart rate. (See page 141 in chapter 7 if you need a reminder on calculating this.) As mentioned in chapter 8, this intensity is based on you being aerobically active on a regular basis. Choose a lower limit when going for a longer duration than 30 minutes. The highest intensity will be brief during the options like intervals, jumps, and variation of uphill techniques provided in this chapter. For most of us, 94 percent of maximum heart rate will take us into an anaerobic stage and thus we would only be able to be there for a brief time. The best way to find out your individual heart rate zone is to schedule a max or submaximal walking test with a health and fitness professional.

Except for changing the surfaces (asphalt, grass, and sand, unless available in the environment), all the other intensifiers in urban Nordic walking can be applied here. When you step up the intensity with the additional pole techniques, it is a good idea to try just one technique at a time. Save something for the next Nordic trail walking adventure. Following are some intensifiers you can experiment with as you go Nordic trail walking during dry conditions as well as during the dry season.

Changing Intensity With Surfaces

The surface on a mountain trail offers a challenge. It might not be an increase in intensity, as sand would offer, but your intense focus on where you step adds to the challenge. The marked trails you choose are most likely maintained and thus you can focus more on the fun of the workout. Safely remove the asphalt paw to expose the spike tip, which will provide good traction in the dirt. If you run into parts that are rocky or have loose gravel, be prepared by strengthening your ankles. The strength training in chapter 2 gives you some good alternative exercises to challenge your balance. Anything that trains your balance, such as standing on one leg, will make those ankles stronger. With more stable ankles you can get through rocky and loose gravel areas much more swiftly.

Changing Intensity With Intervals and Jumps

Apply the one- to five-minute bouts of changing speed (interval training), as you did in chapter 8. Keep the intensity moderate or high during the increased speed and keep the resting part low in intensity. Review the specific examples in chapter 8.

TECHNIQUE TIP

- Vary intensity by changing surfaces: dirt, rocks, loose gravel.
- Vary intensity by changing speed and adding jumps.

Increased speed is an intensifier. The natural tendency after you can't walk any faster is to start jogging or running. Use this tendency to try some low jumps, meaning you stay close to the ground (see figure 9.1). The focus is not on jumping high but on jumping far. Unless you are Superman, you cannot keep this up for very long, so do it for just 15 to 30 seconds. Make sure you perform these jumps on even ground to avoid twisting your ankles. Sometimes it is easier to get into this jumping, flying, and bouncing mode if there is a slight incline.

Figure 9.1 Flying through the trails.

Changing Intensity With Terrain

As with rocky and loose gravel, the unevenness of rugged terrain provides a challenge in itself because you have to stay so focused on where you step.

Nordic trail walking should offer some opportunities to explore the increased intensity of hill training—steeper and longer hills. There are even places in Europe where people compete in Nordic hill walking, which involves climbing one long and steep hill. There are many opinions about competing or not competing in Nordic walking. Since you walk faster without poles, a flat course would not be the best way to compete with Nordic walking. It is still a great way to complete 5Ks, 10Ks, half marathons, or even full marathons. I coach people all the time for those races. The intention may vary, though; some want to compete with themselves to keep track of their progress, some want to use it as a goal, and some want to contribute to a charity to increase the awareness of a specific cause. If you regard it as pure competition, the question is this: Would you have walked faster without the poles? Also, the purpose of Nordic walking is not to walk as fast as possible, but to use the poles correctly to gain

TECHNIQUE TIP

Vary intensity by changing terrain and uphill technique: rugged terrain, hills, and some different ways of climbing the hills.

the benefits. If you focus on walking as fast as possible with the poles, you might lose the technique and thus some of the benefits. Now, a competition up a challenging hill may be more of a true competition since it feels like less of an effort to walk up with poles. However, you can also argue that if you use the full-fledged Nordic walking technique, you will waste so much energy that in the end it is better to pull back on the technique to save some energy if it is a long and steep hill that may take more than 60 minutes. Whether you want to compete or not, hill training is an excellent way of getting in shape fast.

Changing Intensity With Uphill Techniques

In chapter 6, you learned a Nordic walking uphill technique that is similar to Nordic walking on flat surface. The main difference is the intensity. To further intensify your uphill workout, try out the following two ways, which are *not* similar to the regular Nordic walking technique: plant/push back both poles at the same time and skate jump from side to side.

Plant and Push Back Both Poles Simultaneously

A fun and challenging way to go uphill with poles is to plant them at the same time (see figure 9.2*a*). Step forward with the same foot as you plant both poles simultaneously in front of you. This way you will have finished the complete arm movement (see figure 9.2*b*) after you finish a complete stride. Change feet after 15 repetitions. Nordic blading (in-line skating with poles) and skating-style Nordic fitness skiing also involve simultaneous planting of the poles.

Figure 9.2 Try planting and pushing back both poles at the same time while going uphill.

Skate and Jump From Side to Side

This way of going uphill literally feels like you are skating uphill. Instead of planting the pole straight in front of you, plant it out to the side, still in front of you (see figure 9.3). Let the opposite foot follow to the other side. If you add a little bouncing to the movement, you will get into a better rhythm, though it will be more difficult. Try it for 15 to 30 seconds and then return to regular Nordic walking up the hill.

Figure 9.3   Skate and jump from side to side.

Changing Intensity With Nordic Walking Techniques

These last two intensifiers (push back past the hip and open the hand) focus both on the poles and on the body to enhance the workout. If you feel you are ready to add on where you left off from chapter 8, then try them out. Otherwise the examples may only become distractions instead of useful tools to take the workout up a level. Experiment with one example at a time. Let the body become accustomed to the new instructions for a few Nordic walking workouts. When it feels natural and automatic, meaning you don't have to think, then you are ready to apply the next example. These tools are definitely

TECHNIQUE TIP

Vary intensity by adding Nordic walking techniques: Push the hand back *past* the hip, straighten the arm, and open the hand fully.

not limited to the trails. Try them out (one at a time) next time you go for a Nordic walking jaunt in the city.

Push Hand Back Past the Hip and Straighten Arm

Since the time you worked on increasing the speed with both the footwork and the forward lean (see chapter 8), you may have already experienced a reaching back of the hand and arm. If not, this is the goal—to push the hand past the hip and to straighten the arm (see figure 9.4). The key is to keep the end of the pole (spike tip or paw) connected to the ground as long as possible before returning to planting. The more you can reach back and straighten the arm (elbow), the more the back of the arms will be engaged. It requires strong triceps, which you can definitely develop while Nordic walking. To complement this back-of-the-arm motion, it is a good idea to look back to chapter 2, which features some strengthening exercises focusing on this movement. Hill training is an additional way to strengthen the back of the arms, provided you focus on straightening them as much as possible on *each* step. The amount of effort you put in will match the result.

Figure 9.4 To get the best workout for the back of your arms, make sure you push the hand back past the hip and straighten the arm.

Open the Hand Fully

If you have mastered the coordination of the squeeze as you plant and the slight release at the end of the pushing phase (chapter 6), opening the hand will be very simple. All you do now is open the hand to a full release at the end of the pushing phase (past the hip) (see figure 9.5). At first it may be a passive open hand, but eventually you should feel it is an active open hand that follows through the movement of straightening the arm so much that the strap feels like part of the reaching action. It should feel like you are handing something to somebody behind you—like handing off a baton in a relay.

Figure 9.5   Releasing the hand relaxes the muscles and gives the movement a follow-through feeling.

Time with the family—no interruptions from cell phones or computers.

NORDIC WALKER TIP

Here are some other Nordic trail walking adventures:

- Vacation at Nordic trail walking places around the world.
- Bring the family.
- Have a picnic in nature after the cool-down stretch at the end of the workout.
- Enjoy Nordic winter walking and Nordic snowshoeing in the winter.

Conclusion

This chapter gives you the tools to further intensify your Nordic walking workout, but that doesn't mean you can't go Nordic walking on a trail in the mountains if you're a beginner. Just use the techniques in basic Nordic walking (Level 1) from chapter 6 and wait to add the intensifiers. Keep a comfortable pace up those hills and enjoy the nature. If you want to take it up a notch, then apply the techniques from urban Nordic walking (Level 2) in chapter 8. And if you want to test what you're made of, apply the techniques from Nordic trail walking (Level 3) in this chapter. All the Nordic walking techniques in this book can be used in any environment. Now it's up to you to safely apply them, practice them, and have fun with them.

Factors and Options in an Urban Nordic Walking Workout

Factors

- [ ] Time: 1 to 3 hours (remember to warm up and cool down)
- [ ] Intensity: 77 to 94 percent of your maximum heart rate

Options

- [ ] Continuous
- [ ] Surfaces: dirt, rocks, loose gravel
- [ ] Intervals of 1- to 5-minute bouts and low and long jumps of 15 to 30 seconds
- [ ] Terrain: rugged terrain, steeper and longer hills.
- [ ] Uphill techniques: change pole rhythm uphill; change direction from side to side uphill
- [ ] Nordic walking techniques: add pushing hand past the hip straightening the arm; open the hand fully at the very end

Appendix A: Resource Guide for Nordic Walking Equipment

Nordic Walking Kits

Nordic Body
www.NordicBody.com

Nordic Walking Pole Brands

Exel
www.exelpoles.com/portal/
Exerstrider
www.walkingpoles.com
Fittrek
www.fittrek.com
Foot Solutions
www.nordicwalkinghq.com
Gabel
http://cms.gabel.it/
Keen-Fit
www.keenfit.com
Leki
www.leki.com/NordicWalking/ (click on Dealer Locator for international distributors)
Pole Walker
https://polewalkabout.com/Shop
Swix Nordic Walking
www.swixsport.com (click on About and choose Contact Us for international distributors)
Western Pole Company
www.discovernordicwalking.com

Nordic Walking Shoe Brands

Asics
www.asics.com/select.html
Chung Shi (Foot Solutions)
www.footsolutions.com
Lowa
www.lowaboots.com

Reebok
www.store.reebok.com (enter Nordic Walking in the Search box)
Saucony
www.saucony.com
Springboost
www.springboost.com

Appendix B: Resource Guide for Nordic Walking Information Worldwide

Nordic Walking Programs Online

Find information on coaching, programs, and seminars for the public.

Nordic Body
www.NordicBody.com

Nordic Walking Organizations

Find information on classes and instructors for the public and certification seminars for fitness professionals.

International

International Nordic Fitness Organization (INFO)
http://nordicfitness.dnv-online.de

International Nordic Walking Association (INWA)
http://inwa.nordicwalking.com (click on Member Associations to find your country)

International Nordic Walking & Fitness Portal
www.nordicfitnessworld.info

United States

American Nordic Walking Association
http://anwa.us

The American Nordic Walking System
www.skiwalking.com

Fiddlehead Fitness (New York)
www.fiddleheadfitness.com

Fittrek
www.fittrek.com

Nordic Pole Walking USA
www.polewalkingusa.com

Nordic Walk Now
www.nordicwalknow.com

Nordic Walk This Way
www.nordicwalkthisway.com

Nordic Walking North America
www.nordicwalkingna.com

Nordic Walking USA
www.nordicwalkingusa.com

North American Nordic Walking
www.nordicwalker.com

Personal Best Personal Training (Massachusetts)
http://nordicwalking.personalbestpersonaltraining.com

Walk Like a Nord
www.walklikeanord.com

Wolfe's Neck Farm (Maine)
www.wolfesneckfarm.org (click Calendar)

Canada

Dovercourt
www.dovercourt.org/hf_specialty.html

Keenfit
www.keenfit.com

Stride Fitness
www.stridefitness.ca

Trailhead
www.trailhead.ca/

Urban Poling
www.urbanpoling.com/index.php

Walking Proud
www.walkingproud.com

United Kingdom

Breathingspace (Scotland)
www.breathingspaceoutdoors.com/events.html#

British Nordic Walking
www.britishnordicwalking.org.uk/

Midlands Nordic Walking
www.midlandsnordicwalking.org/classesnottinghamshire.php

Nordic Fitness Association
www.nordicfitnessassociation.com/

Nordic Walking School UK
www.nordicwalkingyorkshire.co.uk/

Nordic Walking UK
www.nordicwalking.co.uk

Scottish Nordic Walking Association
www.scottishnordicwalkingassociation.co.uk

New Zealand

Nordic Walking Fitness Association
www.nordicwalking.net.nz

Australia

Nordic Academy
www.nordicacademy.com.au

PoleAbout
http://polewalkabout.com

Germany

Das Nordic Walking Portal
http://nordic-walking-infos.de

Deutscher Nordic Walking (DNV)
www.dnv-online.de/cms

Deutsches Walking Institute (DWI)
www.walking.de

German Nordic Fitness Association (GNFA)
www.gnfa-nordic-walking.de/welcome.php

Lauf Schule (see NW Kurse)
www.L-L-H.de

Medical Nordic Walking
www.medical-nordic-walking.de/index.php

Nordic Walking Union (NWU)
www.nwunion.de

Denmark

INWA Denmark
www.inwa.dk

Nordic Walking—Stavgang
www.stavgang.biz

Luxemburg

Nordic & Walk
www.nordicwalking.lu/trainer.html

Nordic-Walking Luxemburg
www.nordic-walking.lu

Belgium

Nordic Walking België
www.nordicwalking.be

Italy

Associazione Nordic Walking Italia
www.anwi.it

Japan

Japan Nordic Fitness Association
http://japan.nordicwalking.com

Holland

Nordic Walking Almere
www.nordicwalkingalmere.nl

Stichting Nordic Walking Nederland (SNWN)
www.nordicwalking.nl/

Slovenia

IntAct
www.intact.si

Nordic Walking Trips

Find hotels and spas that offer Nordic walking as well as arrange Nordic walking trips.

Der Sport Coach (Switzerland)
www.sportcoach.ch/content.php?id=118&action=view&Wid=57

Europe Wander Hotels
www.wanderhotels.com/en/themes/nordicwalking/index.php#hotels

Freeport Clipper Inn (USA)
www.freeportclipperinn.com

Hotel Lumberger Hof (Austria)
www.lumbergerhof.at/en/sommer_pauschalen/nordic-walking08.php

Hotel Victoria (Switzerland)
www.hotel-victoria.ch

InterCityHotel (Germany)
www.intercityhotel.com/aw/InterCityHotel_Frankfurt_Airport/~ypl/?

Nordic Body
www.NordicBody.com

Nordic Fitness Sports Park
www.nordic-fitness-park.de/

Nordic Walking USA
www.nordicwalkingusa.com

NordicWalking4Fun
www.nordicwalking4fun.nl

Saybrook Point Inn (USA)
www.saybrook.com

Sentiers Nordic Walking Nationaux (Luxemburg)
www.nordicwalkingparc.lu

Stoweflake Mountain Resort & Spa (USA)
www.stoweflake.com

Walkaway Nordic Walking Reizen
www.walkaway.nl

Nordic Walking Events

Find information on annual walking events with a Nordic walking division.

United States

Portland Marathon (October)
www.portlandmarathon.org

Canada

Marathon by the Sea (September)
www.marathonbythesea.com/races

United Kingdom

Lakeland Trails (April, May, September, and October)
www.lakelandtrails.org/index.htm

Switzerland

Eiger Nordic Walking Event (July)
www.eigernordicwalking-event.ch

Nordic Walking Event (June)
www.nordicwalking-event.ch

Swiss Walking Event (August)
www.swisswalking.ch

Walking Day (June)
www.walkingday.ch

New Zealand

5 Volcanoes Challenge (August)
www.totalsport.co.nz/events/volcano/index.php

Cool Running (February)
www.coolrunning.co.nz/races/cathaypacific

Rotorua Marathon (April)
www.rotoruamarathon.co.nz

Nordic Walking News

Stay up to date on the Nordic walking business.

Nordic Walking News
www.nordicwalkingnewsonline.com

Nordic Walking USA
www.nordicwalkingusa.com

Outdoor Retail Stores

Find more information about local hikes and outdoor training classes, such as using a map and a compass.

Adventure 16
www.adventure16.com/locationsmap2.html

Adventure Sports Online
www.adventuresportsonline.com/welcome.htm

LL Bean
www.llbean.com/shop/retailStores/index.html?feat=gn

Polar Heart Rate Monitors
www.polarusa.com/us-en/
This Web site is an online store that specializes in heart rate monitors and sports instruments.

REI
www.rei.com/map/store

Sierra Club
www.sierraclub.org
Although the Sierra Club is not a retail store, it is mentioned in chapter 9 as a great resource for finding local hikes with groups.

Sport Chalet
www.sportchalet.com/

Success Checks

Chapter 1

1. Why do you use poles in Nordic walking?
2. What is one of the reasons your posture improves while Nordic walking?
3. List two reasons why Nordic walking is better than exercising on an elliptical trainer.
4. In what year were the first Nordic walking poles made?
5. True or false: Nordic walking burns 20 to 46 percent more calories than regular walking.
6. What would be a good age for kids to try Nordic walking and why?
7. What makes Nordic walking so versatile?
8. What part of the pole makes it possible to Nordic walk on various surfaces?
9. Should the asphalt paw stay on when you Nordic walk on dirt?
10. Can you go Nordic walking in the city?

Chapter 2

1. Is Nordic walking a full-body workout?
2. What muscles are involved in Nordic walking?
    a. calves, legs, buttocks, abdomen, chest, back, arms, shoulders, and neck
    b. calves, legs, buttocks
    c. abdomen, chest, back, arms, shoulders, and neck
3. What determines the range of motion of a joint?
    a. the extensibility of the muscles
    b. the extensibility of the tendons and the ligaments
    c. the extensibility of all soft tissues (muscles, tendons, ligaments)
4. Which is (are) true?
    a. Muscles attach to bones.
    b. Muscles move bones.
    c. Bones move bones.

5. Which of the following forms of stretching is best to do *after* a workout?

   a. trigger release

   b. dynamic stretching

   c. static stretching

6. What are some of the benefits of strength training?

   a. It improves bone mass.

   b. It improves muscle mass and appearance.

   c. It improves functional fitness.

   d. It improves bone mass, muscle mass, appearance, and functional fitness.

7. What are the three things you want to keep in mind in order to keep good form while exercising?

8. True or false: To get the desired results from strength training, you need to load the muscle enough to become fatigued after a certain number of repetitions.

9. What is the recommendation for improving aerobic capacity?

   a. 10 to 30 minutes, 5 days a week at a moderate to high intensity

   b. 20 to 60 minutes, 3 to 5 days a week at a moderate to high intensity

   c. 40 to 60 minutes, 3 days a week at a moderate to high intensity

10. List at least three benefits of endurance training such as Nordic walking.

Chapter 3

1. What poles can you use for Nordic walking?

   a. trekking poles

   b. downhill skiing poles

   c. Nordic walking poles

2. What is the main difference between the strap of a Nordic walking pole and a trekking pole?

3. List at least three factors of Nordic walking poles that you need to consider when you purchase a pair.

4. What are the benefits of a pole strap that is correctly adjusted to fit your hand snugly?

   a. It gives the hand maximal support in the transfer of power from the planting phase through the push-back phase.

   b. It provides support for the hand, which allows you to only hold on lightly to the grip of the pole.

   c. In the advanced Nordic walking technique, when you release the hand at the end of the push-back phase, the pole can become an extension of your arm.

5. What are some features of a good walking shoe?
   a. flexible front, support under the midfoot, and a rounded heel
   b. stiff front, support under the midfoot, and a rounded heel
   c. flexible front, no support under the midfoot, and a rounded heel

6. What is the common feature of all good Nordic walking shoes?
   a. a ribbed sole to provide great traction
   b. the weight of the shoe
   c. the material of the shoe

7. What type of material should you avoid in a sock and why?
   a. Wool is too warm.
   b. Cotton absorbs too much moisture.
   c. Acrylic is too itchy.

8. How should you dress in Nordic walking?
   a. in layers
   b. in a thick jacket
   c. in tight and restricting clothes

9. How many layers would you need on a cold, windy day, and what is their purpose?

10. Which of the following describe(s) a heart rate monitor?
   a. It measures how fast your heart beats per minute. It comes with two units: a belt and a watch.
   b. It measures the heart rate so you can make sure you work out at a safe zone for your heart. It comes with two units: a belt and a watch.
   c. It is a watch worn around the wrist, accompanied by a belt worn around the waist. It makes it possible to read the pulse off the watch instead of having to stop exercising to take the pulse manually.

Chapter 4

1. Where are the best places to go Nordic walking?
   a. on sidewalks in the city
   b. in a grassy park in the city
   c. on a local wide hiking trail
   d. on a sandy beach

2. You are out Nordic hiking at an average speed when you see two signs saying "1 mile (1,609 meters) to the top" and "During the next mile you

will ascend 1,000 feet (305 meters)." *Approximately* how long will that 1 mile take you?

 a. 10 to 20 minutes

 b. 60 to 90 minutes

3. If you haven't acclimatized, above what elevations might you start dealing with high-altitude concerns?

4. What types of trails does this book recommend for Nordic walking and hiking?

 a. wide and well-marked trails

 b. narrow trails

 c. backcountry trails

5. List at least three factors that would be good to know about the walk before you explore a new Nordic walk or hike.

6. When you explore a new Nordic walk or hike, what would be some helpful tools to bring?

 a. watch, map, compass, GPS

 b. watch, map, chair, GPS

 c. measuring tape, map, compass, GPS

7. How can you find information about new walks in a city you'd never visited before?

 a. the city's Web site

 b. the concierge at the hotel

 c. a retail wilderness store

8. What three things do all the seven Nordic walking wonders have in common?

9. How many countries are represented in the seven Nordic walking wonders?

 a. 7

 b. 10

 c. 5

10. There are designated Nordic walking parks in Europe.

 a. true

 b. false

Chapter 5

1. Name at least three things you need to take into consideration about your personal safety when Nordic walking in any environment.

2. True or false: Before starting any exercise regimen, you should consult with your doctor.

3. Regarding safety and precaution, what are some of the items that you should bring on your Nordic walk?

4. How does the body keep its temperature regulated during exercise?

    a. by sweating

    b. by increased heart rate

    c. by decreased blood pressure

5. A water loss of only ____ percent of a person's body weight can be fatal.

    a. 50 to 60

    b. 9 to 12

    c. 20 to 30

6. True or false: You should drink water before, during, and after exercise.

7. Weight loss after an aerobic exercise session is mainly due to water loss. How much fluid should you drink for every pound (half a kilogram) of water lost?

    a. 16 ounces (half a liter)

    b. 1 liter

    c. 2 liters

8. What is hyponatremia?

    a. It is a medical term for dehydration.

    b. It is another word for high blood pressure.

    c. It is a medical condition caused by drinking too much fluid, which can cause an imbalance in the body's fluids and sodium levels.

9. When Nordic walking or hiking in a group on a mountain trail, where should small children be placed?

    a. in the front

    b. in the middle

    c. in the back

10. When you have the spike tip exposed on the pole and you are not Nordic walking, how should you carry the poles?

    a. vertically

    b. horizontally

    c. diagonally

Chapter 6

1. What is the purpose of planting the pole at an angle?

    a. to prevent the body from moving forward

    b. to push on the brakes

    c. to propel the body forward

2. Why is it beneficial to review regular walking techniques when you learn Nordic walking?

   a. Nordic walking is an enhancement of regular walking and it will save you time in learning Nordic walking.

   b. It shows you how different regular walking is compared to Nordic walking.

   c. It is educational.

3. What is basic Nordic walking?

   a. It is the complete Nordic walking technique.

   b. It is the foundation of all other Nordic walking techniques and intensifiers.

   c. It is the advanced Nordic walking technique.

4. Should beginners be exposed to hills in Nordic walking?

   a. yes

   b. no

5. True or false: In Nordic walking downhill, you mainly focus on changing the body position and the weight distribution instead of changing the height of the poles.

6. List at least 3 of the 10 steps in reviewing regular walking technique.

7. What is meant by dragging of the poles?

   a. It is an exercise for finding the natural walking rhythm.

   b. It is part of the finished Nordic walking technique.

   c. It is an ancient Nordic ritual believed to bring better weather.

8. True or false: Do you plant the pole in a handshake position (elbow in front of the body) in Nordic walking?

9. True or false: Do you push the hand to the hip in basic Nordic walking?

10. Why do you soften the grip of the pole at the end of the push-back position?

   a. It looks better.

   b. It gives the muscles a chance to relax.

   c. It avoids blisters.

Chapter 7

1. True or false: Drink 6 to 12 ounces (180-360 ml) of slightly chilled water every 15 to 20 minutes during exercise.

2. When performing any exercises or daily activity, it is important to move the body with good form. What three things does this book recommend?

   a. Pull the abdomen in slightly, keep shoulders gently back and down, and keep the body aligned.

   b. Arch the back, keep the shoulders apart, turn the feet in.

   c. Flatten the back, keep the shoulders together, turn the feet out.

3. What is the purpose of trigger release?

   a. to strengthen the muscles

   b. to release tension in the muscles

   c. to improve speed

4. What is the main purpose of dynamic stretches?

   a. to increase the length of the muscles

   b. to stabilize the ligaments around the joints

   c. to warm up the muscles and joints to prepare the body for the specific activity to be performed

5. True or false: Start Nordic walking from a slow to a comfortable speed. Give it a good 5 to 10 minutes, or until you feel warm, before you increase the intensity and the speed.

6. If you want to improve your aerobic capacity, what are some of the factors you need to take into consideration?

   a. type of activity, duration, frequency, intensity

   b. location, duration, frequency, intensity

   c. type of activity, duration, rest, intensity

7. Which statement(s) is (are) correct?

   a. A 20-year-old person has an estimated maximum heart rate of 200 beats per minute.

   b. A 30-year-old person has an estimated maximum heart rate of 190 beats per minute.

   c. A 40-year-old person has an estimated maximum heart rate of 180 beats per minute.

8. List at least three ways of varying the intensity of your Nordic walking workout.

9. When you get close to finishing your Nordic walking workout, you should

   a. sprint the last 5 minutes before you come to a complete stop

   b. slow down the pace gradually for 5 minutes before you come to a complete stop

   c. come to a complete stop abruptly

10. What is the main purpose of static stretching at the end of a workout?

   a. to shorten the muscles to get them stronger

   b. to lengthen the muscles to their original length or farther if needed

   c. to stabilize the tendons and ligaments

Chapter 8

1. True or false: You don't have to drive to go Nordic walking; you can start the full-body workout right outside your door in the middle of the city.

2. Which of these great motivators can be distractions in traffic and therefore can jeopardize your safety?

   a. listening to your favorite music

   b. engaging in a conversation with your walking buddy

   c. talking on a cell phone

3. Choose the option that can be applied to Nordic walking on grass in a city park.

   a. Safely remove the asphalt paws to expose the spike tip. When not Nordic walking, carry the poles vertically. Keep a distance from people behind you, to your side, and in front of you.

   b. Keep the asphalt paws on. When not Nordic walking, carry the poles vertically. Keep a distance from people behind you, to your side, and in front of you.

   c. Safely remove the asphalt paws to expose the spike tip. When not Nordic walking, carry the poles horizontally. Keep a distance from people behind you, to your side, and in front of you.

4. What is recommended for Nordic walking in soft, deep sand without asphalt paws?

   a. great basic Nordic walking technique and flexible shoulder joints

   b. great basic Nordic walking technique and a strong core

   c. great basic Nordic walking technique and fast speed

5. In this book, what is the main difference between urban Nordic walking and basic Nordic walking?

   a. Urban Nordic walking can be applied only within city limits, whereas basic Nordic walking can be used anywhere.

   b. Urban Nordic walking is a way to intensify the basic Nordic walking technique by adding three more walking techniques (push off with ball of foot, lean forward as one unit, add a slight upper-body rotation).

   c. Urban Nordic walking is an easier way to use the poles compared to basic Nordic walking.

6. Regarding increasing the intensity of the workout, what is the purpose of pushing off with the ball of the foot and activating the buttocks in Nordic walking?

   a. to increase the speed

   b. to increase the flexibility

   c. to increase the stability in the ankles

7. Leaning forward as one unit is part of the urban Nordic walking technique. What is a great way of practicing it?

    a. walking downhill

    b. walking uphill

    c. walking on a flat surface

8. What is beneficial about a slight upper-body rotation in both regular walking and Nordic walking?

    a. It can improve the flexibility in the legs.

    b. It can strengthen the back of the arms.

    c. It can improve the gait (walking form) and release tension in the back, chest, shoulders, and neck.

9. Where does the slight upper-body rotation occur?

    a. solar plexus

    b. hips

    c. shoulders

10. Besides adding more walking techniques, name at least one way to intensify the Nordic walking workout.

Chapter 9

1. Nordic trail walking can also be called

    a. trekking

    b. Nordic walking on trails

    c. Nordic hiking

2. True or false: To add the techniques of Nordic trail walking, you need to be proficient in the techniques of both basic Nordic walking and urban Nordic walking.

3. The most common trail surfaces are dirt, rocks, and loose gravel. Would you keep the asphalt paws on or remove them while on these surfaces?

    a. asphalt paw on

    b. asphalt paw off (spike tip)

4. Regarding safety, which of the following apply to Nordic trail walking?

    a. Stay to one side around corners to avoid downhill mountain bikers.

    b. Give space to passing people.

    c. Keep your gaze 6 to 10 feet ahead to be aware of holes or uneven parts.

    d. Keep a distance from the person in front of you, especially while going uphill.

5. Surfaces such as dirt, rocks, and gravel will provide a challenge. What part of the body needs to be strong and stable to make it possible for you to move swiftly among those specific areas?

   a. arms

   b. legs

   c. ankles

6. A common way to vary the intensity is to change speed (use interval training). What level of intensity does this chapter recommend?

   a. moderate to high intensity during the increased speed and low intensity during the resting part

   b. moderate intensity during the increased speed and low intensity during the resting part

   c. low intensity during the increased speed and moderate intensity during the resting part

7. Another way to vary the intensity is to use low jumps for 15 to 30 seconds. According to this book, how can you more easily get into this jumping, flying, bouncing mode?

   a. on a slight decline

   b. on a slight incline

   c. on flat terrain

8. A fun and challenging way of going uphill is to change pole rhythm. How is that rhythm described in this chapter?

   a. Opposite arm meets opposite leg.

   b. Plant both of the poles at the same time.

   c. Don't use any poles.

9. What does skate and jump from side to side while going uphill mean?

   a. Plant the left pole out to the left side, still in front of you. Step out with the left foot to the right side.

   b. Plant the left pole out to the left side, still in front of you. Step out with the left foot to the left side.

   c. Plant the right pole out to the right side, still in front of you. Step out with the left foot to the left side.

10. Adding the features of Nordic trail walking gives you a complete Nordic walking technique. What are the last two techniques you need to add?

    a. Push the hand past the hip (elbow is straight) and open the hand at the very end.

    b. Plant the pole in a handshake position and lean forward as one unit.

    c. Push the hand at least to the hip and soften the grip on the pole.

Chapter 1 Answers

1. You use poles to engage the muscles in the upper body.

2. The second you place the poles on the ground, you improve your posture—you push away from gravity.

3.
   a. The poles are measured to match your height. The elliptical trainer cannot be changed whether you are 6 feet tall or 5 feet tall.

   b. On an elliptical trainer, the arms are bent the whole time, and the machine mainly works muscles crossing the shoulder joint, such as the chest and the back muscles. The poles allow you to straighten the elbow behind you, which shapes the back of your arms (the triceps).

4. 1997

5. true

6. The age of 10 would be a good introduction age mainly because of one aspect of child development: coordination.

7. You can Nordic walk anywhere because you can use the poles on any surface: asphalt, grass, dirt, sand, snow, and ice.

8. the removable asphalt paw at the end of the pole

9. no

10. yes

Chapter 2 Answers

1. yes

2. a

3. c

4. a and b

5. c

6. d

7. Keep the abdomen lightly pulled in, keep the shoulders gently back and down, and keep the body aligned.

8. true

9. b

10. increased aerobic capacity; reduced risk of cardiovascular diseases (heart attack, stroke); reduced risk of type 2 diabetes; improved stamina; less fatigue; ease in doing daily activities; improved resting blood pressure; decreased total cholesterol; increased HDL (good cholesterol); decreased body fat

Chapter 3 Answers

1. c
2. All Nordic walking poles (except the strapless Exerstrider poles) have an adjustable strap that supports the whole hand. The trekking pole has a simple loop as a strap.
3. length of the pole, the strap, the grip, the shaft, the spike tip, the asphalt paw
4. a, b, and c
5. a
6. a
7. b
8. a
9. Three layers. The first layer is for ventilation. It's the one that will be the closest to the skin, and it takes moisture away from the skin either to keep the body warm or to keep it cool. The second layer is for insulation. The third layer is for protection from wind and water.
10. a, b, and c

Chapter 4 Answers

1. a, b, c, and d
2. b
3. 8,000 feet (2,438 m) above sea level
4. a
5. distance, time, elevation, and terrain
6. a
7. a, b, and c
8. They all describe a walk in the city, a walk in a park or on a beach, and a local hike.
9. c (USA, Canada, Japan, New Zealand, and Sweden)
10. a

Chapter 5 Answers

1. the condition of your health, what items you bring, how much water and food you pack, how you dress for the weather, and how you act and react in the city as well as in the mountains

2. true

3. a fully charged cell phone, a current ID, a note with contact information to three local people in case of an emergency, some cash, and a valid credit card

4. a

5. b

6. true

7. a

8. c

9. b

10. a

Chapter 6 Answers

1. c

2. a

3. b

4. a

5. true

6. heel strikes first, rock and roll like a rocker, heel comes off the ground, push off with the ball of the foot, activate the buttocks, fall (lean) forward, opposite arm meets opposite leg, use an even and straight arm swing, use a slight twist of the torso, use balanced walking

7. a

8. true

9. true

10. b

Chapter 7 Answers

1. true

2. a

3. b

4. c

5. true

6. a

7. a, b, and c

8. Use intervals: vary speed and intensity in 1- to 5-minute bouts. Change surfaces: asphalt, grass, dirt, soft sand. Change terrain: flat land and hills. Change techniques: basic Nordic walking technique, the technique intensifiers of urban Nordic walking and Nordic trail walking.

9. b

10. b

Chapter 8 Answers

1. true
2. a, b, and c
3. a
4. b
5. b
6. a
7. b
8. c
9. a
10. Change surfaces (from asphalt to grass and sand), use hills, use intervals.

Chapter 9 Answers

1. b and c
2. true
3. b
4. a, b, c, and d
5. c
6. a
7. b
8. b
9. c
10. a

Photo Credits

AP Images

AP Photo/Graham Morrison   Page 1

AP Photo/Jens Meyer   Page 7

Art Explosion   Page 54, 70, 102, 112, 119, 163

Courtesy of Paula Artley   Page 81, 82

Getty Images

Hermann Erber/LOOK/Getty Images (top left)   Page 17

Photodisc/Getty Images (bottom left)   Page 17

Photodisc/Getty Images (bottom right)   Page 17

Icon

Schne/Imago/Icon SMI (bottom right)   Page 16

JEAN-NOEL HERRANZ/DPPI/Icon SMI (top right)   Page 17

Eisend/Imago/Icon SMI   Page 19

San Diego Union-Tribune/Zuma Press/Icon SMI   Page 111

Courtesy of Marilyn Inch   Page 85

Courtesy of Gary Johnson   Page 78, 79 (both photos)

Courtesy of June Stevenson   Page 87, 88, 89

Malin Svensson   Page 16 (top right), 67, 74, 75, 76, 93, 94, 95

Courtesy of Naohiro Takahashi   Page 91 (both photos), 92

Courtesy of Tourism Saint John, New Brunswick, Canada   Page 84

Bibliography

Chapter 1

Bumgardner, W. 2008. Exerstriding vs. Nordic walking techniques. http://walking.about.com/od/exerstriding/a/exerstrider.htm.

Church. T. 2001. *Exel Nordic walking* [video].

Fittrek. N.d. Nordic walking techniques–How to get started. www.fittrek.com/howto.htm.

Svensson, M. 2008. *Malin's method for weight loss*. Santa Monica, CA: Author.

SWR Fernsehen activ. N.d. Nordic walking: Der Alf-technik. www.swr.de/aktiv/walking/training/beitrag4.html.

Benefits and Studies

Anttila, R., S. Holopainen, and Jokinen. 1999. Pole walking and the effect of regular 12-week pole walking exercise on neck and shoulder symptoms: The mobility of the cervical and thoracic spine and aerobic capacity. Final project work for the Helsinki IV College for health care professionals.

Baatile J., W.E. Langbein, F. Weaver, C. Maloney, and M.B. Jost. September/October 2000. Effect of exercise on perceived quality of life of individuals with Parkinson's disease. *Journal of Rehabilitation Research and Development* 37(5): 529-34.

Church, T.S., C.P. Earnest, and G.M. Morss. September 2002. Field testing of physiological responses associated with Nordic walking. *Research Quarterly for Exercise and Sport* 73(3): 296-300.

Collins E.G., W.E. Langbein, C. Orebaugh, C. Bammert, K. Hanson, D. Reda, L.C. Edwards, and F.N. Littooy. 2003. Polestriding exercise and vitamin E for management of peripheral vascular disease. *Medicine & Science in Sports & Exercise* 35(3): 384-393.

Generation Fit. N.d. Cross lateral movement organizes brain functions. www.generation-fit.com/0_readingfirst.asp.

Jordan, A.N., T. Olson, C.P. Earnest, G. Morss, and T.S. Church. May 2001. Metabolic cost of high intensity poling while Nordic walking versus normal walking. *Medicine & Science in Sports & Exercise* 33(5) (Supplement 1):S86.

Karvonen, M., and V. Tolppala. 2001. The effects of stick walking on neck and shoulder pain in office workers. Final project work at Mikkeli Polytechnic School degree programme of physiotherapy.

Morss, G M., T.S. Church, C.P. Earnest, and A.N. Jordan. May 2001. Field test comparing the metabolic cost of normal walking versus walking with Nordic walking. *Medicine & Science in Sports & Exercise* 33(5) (Supplement 1):S23.

Parkatti T., T. Tikkanen, and M. Kauppi. 2002. Ikääntyvän työntekijän työssä jaksaminen: työnkehittämisohjelma ja sen vaikuttavuus. *Gerontologia* 16:74-81.

Ripatti, T. 2002. Effect of Nordic walking training program on cardiovascular fitness. Academic degree study. Köln, Germany: Sportartspezifische Leistungsfähigkeit Deutsche Sportshochschule.

Schwameder, H., R. Roithner, E. Muller, W. Niessen, and C. Raschner. December 1999. Knee joint forces during downhill walking with hiking poles. *Journal of Sports Sciences* 17(12): 969-978.

Shape Up America. 2008. Caloric expenditure for walking. www.shapeup.org/interactive/phys1.php.

Stoughton, L.K. 1992. Psychological profiles before and after 12 weeks of walking or Exerstrider training in adult women. Thesis. University of Wisconsin at La Crosse.

Svensson, M. 2003. *Nordic Walking USA Basic Instructor Manual.* Santa Monica, CA: Author.

Walter P.R., J.P. Porcari, G. Brice, and L. Terry. 1996. Acute responses to using walking poles in patients with coronary artery disease. *Journal of Cardiopulmonary Rehabilitation* 16(4): 245-50.

Willson, J., M.R. Torry, M.J. Decker, T. Kernozek, and J.R. Steadman. January 2001. Effects of walking poles on lower extremity gait mechanics. *Medicine & Science in Sports & Exercise* 33 (1): 142-147.

Chapter 2

Flexibility

Clark, M.A., and R.J. Corn. 2001. *NASM OPT optimum performance training for the fitness professional.* 1st ed. Thousand Oaks, CA: National Academy of Sports Medicine.

Howley, E.T., and B.D. Franks. 2007. *Fitness professional's handbook.* 5th ed. Champaign, IL: Human Kinetics.

National Strength and Conditioning Association. Baechle, T.R. (Ed.). 1994. *Essentials of strength training and conditioning.* Champaign, IL: Human Kinetics.

Trigger Release

Gach, M.R. 2008. Introduction to acupressure. www.acupressure.com/articles/introacu.htm.

Dynamic Stretching

American College of Sports Medicine. 2006. *ACSM's resource manual for guidelines for exercise testing and prescription.* 5th ed. Baltimore: Lippincott Williams & Wilkins.

Clark, M.A., and R.J. Corn. 2001. *NASM OPT optimum performance training for the fitness professional.* 1st ed. Thousand Oaks, CA: National Academy of Sports Medicine.

Fowles, J.R., D.G. Sale, and J.D. MacDougall. 2000. *Reduced strength after passive stretch of the human plantar flexors.* Study used in lecture by Piotr Wroblewski, INWA (International Nordic Walking Association) 2006 Convention, Poland.

Static Stretching

American College of Sports Medicine. 2006. *ACSM's resource manual for guidelines for exercise testing and prescription*. 5th ed. Baltimore: Lippincott Williams & Wilkins.

Benefits and Types of Strength Training

American College of Sports Medicine. 2006. *ACSM's resource manual for guidelines for exercise testing and prescription*. 5th ed. Baltimore: Lippincott Williams & Wilkins.

Peak Bone Mass

Bodybuilding judging criteria. N.d. www.exrx.net/Bodybuilding/JudgingCriteria.html.

Howley, Edward T. and B. Don Franks. 2007. *Fitness professional's handbook*. 5th ed. Champaign, IL: Human Kinetics.

Endurance Training

American College of Sports Medicine. 2006. *ACSM's resource manual for guidelines for exercise testing and prescription*. 5th ed. Baltimore: Lippincott Williams & Wilkins.

Fitness Gatherings. 2008. Benefits of cardiorespiratory exercise. www.fitnessgatherings.com/benefits%20cardio.htm.

Rockwood School District. N.d. Benefits of cardiorespiratory exercise. www.rockwood.k12.mo.us/fitness/Fitness_Concepts_page.htm#Benefits_of_Exercise_.

Wilmore, J.H., and D.L. Costill. 1999. *Physiology of sport and exercise*. 2nd ed. Champaign, IL: Human Kinetics.

Chapter 3

SunriseWD. 2008. Corn plastic water bottle. www.sunrisewd.com/products/1liter_bottle.htm.

Svensson, M. 2008. *Malins method for weight loss*. Santa Monica, CA: Author.

Chapter 4

INet Tours. 2008. Golden Gate Park San Francisco Pictures and History. www.inetours.com/Pages/SFNbrhds/Golden_Gate_Park.html.

Wikipedia. N.d. New Brunswick, Canada. http://en.wikipedia.org/wiki/New_Brunswick.

Wikipedia. N.d. North Island, New Zealand. http://en.wikipedia.org/wiki/North_Island.

Wikipedia. N.d. Santa Monica, California. http://en.wikipedia.org/wiki/Santa_Monica,_California.

Wikipedia. N.d. Transportation in Portland, Oregon. http://en.wikipedia.org/wiki/Portland,_Oregon#Transportation.

Wilderness Education Association (WEA). Goldenberg, M., and B. Martin, (Eds.) 2008. *Outdoor adventures: Hiking and backpacking.* Champaign, IL: Human Kinetics.

Chapter 5

Fluid and Energy Replacement

About.com. N.d. Eating after exercise. http://sportsmedicine.about.com/cs/nutrition/a/aa081403.htm.

American College of Sports Medicine. 2006. *ACSM's guidelines for exercise testing and prescription.* 7th ed. Baltimore: Lippincott Williams & Wilkins.

American College of Sports Medicine. 2006. *ACSM's resource manual for guidelines for exercise testing and prescription.* 5th ed. Baltimore: Lippincott Williams & Wilkins.

Howley, E.T., and B.D. Franks. 2007. *Fitness professional's handbook.* 5th ed. Champaign, IL: Human Kinetics.

Wikipedia. N.d. Hyponatremia. http://en.wikipedia.org/wiki/Hyponatremia.

Wilmore, J.H., and D.L. Costill. 1999. *Physiology of sport and exercise.* 2nd ed. Champaign, IL: Human Kinetics.

Trail Safety

About.com. N.d. Blister prevention and treatment guide. http://sportsmedicine.about.com/cs/foot_facts/a/aa031400a.htm.

Wilderness Education Association (WEA). Goldenberg, M., and B. Martin. (Eds.). 2008. *Hiking and backpacking.* Champaign, IL: Human Kinetics.

Pole Safety

Svensson, M. 2008. *Malin's method for weight loss.* Santa Monica, CA: Author.

Wildlife Etiquette

Hachmeister, M.E. 1993. Mountain lion. www.northern.edu/natsource/ENDANG1/Mounta1.htm.

Chapter 6

Svensson, M. 2008. *Malin's method for weight loss.* Santa Monica, CA: Author.

Chapter 7

Warm-Up and Cool-Down

American College of Sports Medicine. 2006. *ACSM's guidelines for exercise testing and prescription.* 7th ed. Philadelphia: Lippincott Williams & Wilkins.

Factors Improving Aerobic Capacity

American College of Sports Medicine. 2006. *ACSM's guidelines for exercise testing and prescription*. 7th ed. Philadelphia: Lippincott Williams & Wilkins.

Chapter 8

Intensity

American College of Sports Medicine. 2006. *ACSM's guidelines for exercise testing and prescription*. 7th ed. Philadelphia: Lippincott Williams & Wilkins.

About the Author

Malin Svensson is internationally recognized as one of the leading authorities on Nordic walking. She is a certified international coach through the International Nordic Walking Association (INWA) and is one of only four individuals, and the first female, to obtain this prestigious certification. Also a certified personal trainer (NSCA and NASM), Svensson is founder of Nordic Walking USA and founder and owner of Nordic Body. Malin holds a master's degree in physical education and is a nationally ranked track and field athlete.

As a fitness speaker and coach, Svensson has conducted Nordic walking seminars and presentations throughout North America, Europe, and New Zealand. Her writing on Nordic walking has been featured in the *Los Angeles Times, New York Times, Wall Street Journal, Fitness, Body+Soul, Weight Watchers,* and *All You.*

Svensson is the author of the *Nordic Walking Instructor Manual* and coauthor of the *INWA Instructor Manual.* She is also cohost of the *Exel Nordic Walking DVD* along with Mark Fenton. She is a member of INWA Advisory Board and has served on the INWA Educational Committee and as director of education of Exel Sport North America.

A native of Sweden, Svensson moved to the United States in 1989. She resides in Santa Monica, California, where she enjoys Nordic walking in the walking friendly city and in the Santa Monica Mountains. Travel and improvisational theater are also favorite leisure pursuits.

Need more adventure?

Want to go canoeing, kayaking, hiking, rock climbing, or Nordic walking? Start today with the Outdoor Adventures series. This practical series provides you with the essential information to get ready and go. The Outdoor Adventures series is designed to prepare you with instruction in the basic techniques and skills so you can be on your way to an adventure in no time.

Hiking and Backpacking
by the Wilderness Education Association

Canoeing
by the American Canoe Association

Kayaking
by the American Canoe Association

Rock Climbing
by the Wilderness Education Association

Nordic Walking
by Malin Svensson

To learn more about the books in this series, visit the Outdoor Adventures series Web site at **www.HumanKinetics.com/OutdoorAdventures**.

For a complete description or to order
Call **1-800-747-4457**
In Canada, call **1-800-465-7301**
In Europe, call **44 (0) 113-255-5665**
In Australia, call **08-8372-0999**
In New Zealand, call **09-448-1207**

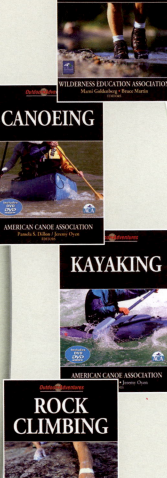

 HUMAN KINETICS
The Information Leader in Physical Activity